"Happy Fondues" Darli___ __2)

Le Creuset's

FONDUE COOKERY

Le Creuset's

FONDUE COOKERY

WENDY VEALE

MARTIN BOOKS

Design: Patrick McLeavey & Partners
Photography: Laurie Evans
Styling: Lesley Richardson
Food preparation for photography: Allyson Birch
Typesetting: Ace Filmsetting Ltd, Frome, Somerset
Printed and bound by Cayfosa Industria Grafica, Spain

Published by Martin Books
Simon & Schuster Consumer Group
Fitzwilliam House
32 Trumpington Street
Cambridge CB2 1QY

in association with Le Creuset
The Kitchenware Merchants Ltd
4 Stephenson Close
East Portway Andover
Hampshire SP10 3RU

First published 1991
© The Kitchenware Merchants Ltd 1991
ISBN 0 85941 741 7

With thanks to Sue Cutts, home economist for Le Creuset

RECIPE NOTES
All measures are level. All eggs are medium (size 3) unless otherwise stated.
Measurements are given in both metric and imperial units: do not mix metric
and imperial measurements in any one recipe as they are not interchangeable.

Pictured on the front cover: Fondue Savoyarde (page 15) with Gruyère Moons (page 116)
Pictured on the title page: Fruits of the Forest Fondue (page 60)

CONTENTS

FOREWORD

Like so many good ideas, the original Le Creuset Fondue Set evolved from one person's enthusiasm for something new. Little did he know that some thirty years on so many people all over the world would enjoy the companionship, variety and wealth of flavours that fondue cookery can bring. This aspiring Le Creuset employee returned from an exhilarating holiday in Switzerland full of enthusiasm, not just for skiing and the après-ski entertainments, but full of fondues – in every sense.

Fondue cookery is centuries old, and by the 1800s ideas were being passed between food connoisseurs, who were creating recipes not just with Swiss cheeses, but with French and Italian ones too. Vegetable and egg fondues were also created.

However, these very early fondues lacked the facility to keep the fondue pot hot at the table after it was prepared in the kitchen. Early fondue participants had to be at the ready, forks and bread in hand, so they could start eating quickly before the mixture cooled. Often the pot had to be returned to the kitchen, or fire, to reheat.

We do not know quite what method of keeping the fondue pot hot our Le Creuset scout found in Switzerland, but not long after his return the first Le Creuset Fondue Set was on the market. A cast-iron pot, a stable cast-iron stand and its own small burner to keep the fondue at just the right consistency and temperature, was the simple but so effective arrangement.

In developing this new product, Le Creuset already had the expertise of casting cookware products in all shapes and sizes. Cast iron was then, and still is, recognised to be an ideal cooking material, and its attributes are well suited to the requirements of the fondue. It has good, even heat absorption and distribution and can be used equally well on very low heats, required for cheese fondues; as well as higher settings, such as those required for meat and fish fondues. Cast iron can be used on all heat sources, which is of vital importance as most fondues begin by a degree of preparation on the hob. Once hot, cast iron retains heat extremely well, so is ideally suited to being kept warm over a very gentle flame.

Today Le Creuset Fondue Sets are sold all over the world and a variety of designs and colours are available. Some are dual-purpose, making them suitable for cheese, meat, fish, vegetable and dessert fondues, whilst others are of a specialist nature. The 'cheese fondue set' has a wider, shallow pot so that large quantities of cheese melt very easily, whilst the 'chocolate fondue set' could be the answer to a chocoholic's dream, keeping chocolate, laced with cream and a favourite liqueur, melted and warm for hours.

Whatever the occasion, a fondue makes a grand centrepiece and talking point. It can be informal, sophisticated, very sociable and fun, but most importantly, as the recipes in this book illustrate, simplicity itself to prepare.

Bon Appetit! Le Creuset

INTRODUCTION

Mention the word 'fondue' and it may call to mind glowing après-ski evenings in the Alps, soothing weary limbs with tumblers of warm glühwein and gathering round the bubbling fondue pot to share a meal steeped in tradition and symbolic of friendship.

. . . Or, it may conjure up memories closer to home – an informal get-together with friends, or a hazy recollection of a hot summer's day skewering sizzling barbecued meats into a simmering fondue sauce.

. . . But, alas, for some of us it is a time for admission. If only we had known what to do with the wedding present from cousin Pierre, or could remember which cupboard that house-warming gift was hiding in! We have missed a simple, pleasant way of sharing food.

A glance through this book tells its own story. Fondues are fun – for the family and for friends. Fondues make sociable gatherings easy and simple. Food preparation takes on a new lease of life, and encourages the whole household to spend time together over a meal, because the merest hint of a fondue lunch or supper summons hungry appetites and even willing hands to the table!

Whether preparing a simple Saturday brunch for the family, or fortifying weary children home from school, or partying to celebrate birthdays and festivals, one thing will become apparent: the Le Creuset Fondue Set will join the privileged kitchen equipment on the work surface – and within arm's reach!

Fondues . . . for the family, for fun . . . from Le Creuset.

THE HISTORY OF THE FONDUE

Today, the fondue is the national dish of Switzerland, but many variations are enjoyed throughout the world. A glance back in time reveals that fondues originated several hundred years ago and evolved because of the geography and climate of their native country.

During the cold Alpine winters, snow-covered mountains and valleys cut off the small villages from the towns and, consequently, fresh food became scarce. The villagers had to rely upon locally made produce, which included cheeses, bread and wine. As the winter wore on, so the wheels of cheese, produced by the valley cheesemakers in the summer months, became drier and more unpalatable. Out of necessity came a marvellous dish – the fondue. The name derives from the French verb *fondre* meaning 'to melt' or 'to blend' – and this was precisely what the stale cheese needed to make it more digestible. The cheese was melted in an earthenware pot called a *caquelon*, local wine and seasonings were added and even the stale bread tasted delicious after it was swirled into the simmering cheese sauce.

Although communal eating from one pot implied a shortage of cooking equipment and utensils amongst the poorer peasants, it was also symbolic of 'community dining' – each participant keeping to his corner of the pot, showing consideration and friendship – a Swiss custom still respected to this day.

The traditional Swiss fondue recipe was named after the region of Neuchâtel and used Gruyère and Emmental cheeses, but very soon the remaining regions (or cantons) in Switzerland created their own variations, using local cheeses and wines. Ingredients like ham, eggs and tomatoes were added and, as the fondue spread into neighbouring countries, further variations developed.

In Italy, the fonduta was created – made with the local fontina cheese and eggs, enhanced with white truffles from the Piedmont. The Italians ladled the fonduta over slabs of polenta – a cornmeal dish dating back to the times of the Romans. Meanwhile, in France, the town of Aubusson developed its *fondu* using local cheeses and wine and served with chunks of potato. The eighteenth-century gastronome Brillat-Savarin was given a fondue recipe by a Swiss friend. This he published in *The Physiology of Taste* in 1824, which spread the word even further afield. Although his recipe involved scrambled eggs and cheese, it still required the same principle of melting and blending the ingredients together. The famous Larousse Gastronomique dictionary of food and cooking described a fondue as a vegetable preparation cooked in butter or oil for a long time until reduced to a pulp.

TRADITIONS AND FORFEITS

Switzerland still recognises the Fondue Neuchâtel as its national dish, and the Swiss make a point of enjoying fondue evenings with family and friends from neighbouring farms and dairies. The fondue is traditionally enjoyed during the months of October to April because outdoor work finishes earlier in the day, and the long evenings give the cheesemakers, herdsmen and dairy farmers time to relax. What better way to pass a cold winter's evening than around a warming fondue?

Sharing the fun of a fondue evening can be full of surprises! There are usually forfeits to be paid whether the fondue is eaten in a local restaurant or a home. Even the seasoned fondue eater, while swirling his crust of bread in the shape of a figure eight (to keep the fondue creamy) may accidentally lose it in the fondue. If this happens, be warned! A woman will pay with a kiss to all the gentlemen present, a man must provide a bottle of wine or give the hostess a glass of kirsch – and, if either party makes the same mistake again, they will have to host the next fondue party . . . !

The choice of drinks at a fondue party is debatable. It is the custom not to drink during a fondue, but a glass of 'kirschwasser' or cherry brandy taken half-way through the proceedings is known as a *coup de mileau*. Expert fondue-eaters also enjoy dipping their bread into 'kirschwasser' before it goes into the fondue.

Cold drinks combined with the warm cheese fondue were thought to cause indigestion, hence the tradition of drinking unsweetened tea, a small glass of schnapps, warm fruit juices or glühwein – or the same dry wine, usually a Hock or Riesling, that had been used in the fondue dish – served at room temperature, rather than chilled as normal.

During the time it takes for five or six people to share a fondue, a great delicacy is formed. This is found at the bottom of the fondue pot once the last trace of cheese has been mopped up. The croûton – a brown crust – is ceremoniously flambéed in 'kirschwasser', before the host scrapes it off the base and shares it among the guests. Incidentally, it is also known as the *religieuse* – probably because the sharing of it is almost as serious as a religious ceremony!

MAKING YOUR OWN FONDUES

Fondue recipes can be endless, thanks to the vast range of ingredients – local and continental cheeses and wines, exotic varieties of fruits and vegetables – we now have on our doorstep. These, combined with the simplicity of fondue cooking, will prove a constant temptation to adapt recipes and create fresh ideas.

However, for each type of fondue – cheese, meat or fish and dessert – there are general guidelines. One of these is timing. As a rule of thumb (from start of cooking), a cheese fondue takes 15–20 minutes, meat and fish (once oil has heated) 5 minutes, and a dessert fondue 10 minutes or less.

THE CHEESE FONDUE

• By using the Le Creuset cast-iron fondue pan, successful results will always be achieved – the steady, even heat of the pan and fine control of the lamp will prevent the cheese from overheating and spoiling.

• Use a mature or flavoursome cheese, coarsely grated, cut into thin slices or diced. Bear in mind that the dryness of a cheese will affect the final consistency of the fondue.

• The acidity of lemon juice helps the cheese to melt smoothly. Add 1 teaspoon to your recipe.

• Always choose a dry white wine or cider. If in doubt about its dryness, add a teaspoon of lemon juice. Heat the wine before adding it, to make the cheese melt more quickly.

• Melt the cheese slowly, over a low heat. Do not allow it to boil or it will become stringy. Once the fondue pan is transferred to its stand, the fondue should bubble gently.

• Do not worry if the cheese initially separates from the wine – keep stirring and it will soon become smooth and blended.

• If you find the cheese forming a solid lump – which may happen if you add it too quickly – raise the heat slightly and stir continuously: it will eventually become smooth.

• To rescue a curdled fondue, add a few more drops of lemon juice and beat vigorously with a wooden spoon.

• If a cheese fondue becomes too thick, add a drop of warmed wine, or a pinch of bicarbonate of soda. If it becomes too thin, add a little cornflour blended with some liquid or add a little extra grated cheese.

• Allow half a french stick or 175–250 g (6–8 oz) bread for each person. Always leave a piece of crust on the bread to help the fondue fork anchor in it.

- Bread for dipping must not be too fresh, or it will crumble in the fondue. The bread can be baked lightly to make it firmer.

- Take care – a cheese fondue will be very hot to eat.

- Seasoned fondue eaters always stir the fondue whilst dipping their bread, to keep it smooth and free from lumps. Stirring the fondue in the shape of a figure eight is said to represent the cross of the Swiss flag, but it's also a good way of coating your bread thoroughly!

- Foods other than bread can be offered for dipping: baby tomatoes, carrots, celery, button mushrooms, cauliflower florets, savoury biscuits, choux buns, prawns and cooked meats.

- Serve the fondue accompanied by a mulled wine, cider or lemon tea. Alternatively, serve a dry white wine at room temperature; a chilled drink on top of the cheese can cause indigestion!

- Traditionally, cold meats and salads, and a dessert of fresh fruits or an open cherry tart can be offered after the fondue, if there is any room!

- Chill any leftovers before cutting them into cubes and adding to cream of tomato or vegetable soups; or spread them on toast or in jacket potatoes and grill.

———————————— *MEAT AND FISH FONDUES*————————————

- Meat or fish fondues can be cooked in either oil, stock or sherry. The heat-retaining properties of the Le Creuset fondue pan help maintain a constant temperature, giving perfect results.

———————————— *Oil* ————————————

- Never overfill the fondue pan, one-third-full is the maximum because the oil may bubble up when food is added. Heat the oil on the hob and do not leave it unattended.

- An ideal temperature for frying is 190°C/375°F. To check that this temperature has been reached, drop a small cube of bread into the hot oil. It will brown in less than one minute if at the correct temperature.

- For extra flavour add two tablespoons of olive oil and some fresh herbs, such as bay leaves or parsley, to the oil.

———————————— *Stock and Sherry* ————————————

- The fondue pan should be a maximum of half to two-thirds full.

- A bouquet garni, loose fresh herbs, black peppercorns or garlic will enhance the flavour. The leftover stock is full of flavour and can be used in a soup.

——————— *Preparing and Cooking* ———————

• Allow approximately 250 g (8 oz) meat or fish for each person. Choose lean cuts of meat – fillet of beef, sirloin or rump; lean lamb or pork, or chicken. Remind your guests that pork and chicken must be cooked through thoroughly.

• Choose firm fish that will not flake apart on the fork – monkfish, tuna, halibut, mussels, prawns and scallops, for example.

• The meat and fish must be dried thoroughly with kitchen paper towels to prevent the oil from spitting.

• Before cooking the meat or fish, spear the fondue fork right through to extend 5 mm (¼ inch) out on the other side. This will prevent it from sticking to the base of the fondue pan.

• Do not add too much food to the oil at a time, because it will lower the temperature of the oil. The oil will then need reheating on the hob.

• NEVER EAT STRAIGHT FROM THE FONDUE FORK – THE FOOD WILL BE VERY HOT! Transfer the food to a plate and eat with a dinner fork.

• Prepare an assortment of dipping sauces and relishes, and accompany the fondue with salads, coleslaws and breads.

——————— *THE DESSERT FONDUE* ———————

• A wonderful finale to a meal – the Le Creuset chocolate fondue pan will produce a meltingly smooth dessert, but without the risk of burning or scorching on the base.

• If you do not own a chocolate fondue, use an ordinary one but remember to stand the melted chocolate over a *very low* flame to keep warm.

• NEVER BOIL A DESSERT FONDUE RECIPE unless stated in the recipe.

• Allow 250 g (8 oz) chocolate, 150 ml (¼ pint) cream and 2 tablespoons liqueur for 4 persons – as a basic recipe for your own creations.

• Because a fondue eaten as a dessert should not be hot, but just warm, guests will only require the fondue fork for eating.

• Accompany chocolate, and other sweet fondues, with a selection of fresh fruit. Chill the fruit well before serving: the chocolate or fondue will adhere better.

• Nuts (when available) or glacé fruits (pineapple, cherries, etc.) are delicious dipped into the chocolate fondue.

• Sponge squares and fingers, marshmallows, ratafias and macaroons, cubes of flapjack or coconut ice, sweet brioche, tiny choux buns and spiced biscuits and cookies for dipping will add variety and interesting textures.

BEFORE YOU BEGIN YOUR FONDUE

To ensure your fondues are fun, informal and sociable it is worth noting a few simple rules for safety.

• Read the instruction leaflet enclosed in your fondue set, particularly the notes on lighting the burner.

• Always place the fondue stand and burner on a heatproof surface, large mat or tray.

• Always supervise children when the fondue set is in use.

• When refilling the burner with meths or special fondue fuel, remove the vessel to a safe, well-ventilated location, away from flames or other sources of ignition.

• Never refill the lamp whilst very hot or alight.

• Never use a damaged burner, or one with a missing snuffer, air regulator or any other part.

• Take care when moving a hot pot of oil or fondue from the hob to the fondue stand. A cloth should be used for lifting.

—————————— LIGHTING THE BURNER USING METHYLATED SPIRITS ——————————

• Remove the snuffer and fill the lamp with methylated spirit or ethyl alcohol. (These burn with a clear, or bluish, flame.) Fill to the level of the wire lattice (approx. 125 ml/4 fl oz).

• Wipe up any spillage from the edge.

• Put the burner into place on the stand, positioning it so that the handle can move freely for opening or closing the vents.

• Open the vents by moving the handle to the left, apply a match to the central opening. (Hold the match from the side.)

• The level of the flame can be adjusted by gently moving the handle to the right. This closes the vent, reducing the air supply, and the size of the flame.

• As a guideline: 6 air holes open – large flame
3 air holes open – medium flame
all 6 closed – small flame

• Fondue recipes which can burn easily, such as cheese or dessert fondues, should be heated over a small flame.

• To extinguish, close the air holes and replace the snuffer over the burner.

• It is preferable to store the burner empty, replenishing the methylated spirit for each use.

USING SPECIAL FONDUE FUEL

Some fondue sets have burners designed to take special containers of fondue fuel. These burners should only be used with this fuel; methylated spirit or other flammable liquids are not suitable.

The fuel comes in pre-sealed packs with enough fuel to last, usually, for two fondues. After use, and if it is to be kept, the pack should be thoroughly cooled and well sealed to prevent evaporation of the fuel. For more information, see page 126.

• To use, remove the seal from the pack and place the container in the fondue burner. Replace the burner cover and place the burner in the fondue stand.

• Open the burner holes and light the fuel through the central hole. When thoroughly alight, regulate the size of the flame with the burner handle.

• Store unused packs of the fuel in a cool cupboard away from heat sources or any naked flames.

FONDUES
for the
FAMILY

FONDUE SAVOYARDE

(CHEESE FONDUE) SERVES 6–8

This is a traditional cheese fondue which tends to use Gruyère, Comté (a French-style Gruyère cheese) or Emmental. Try experimenting with your favourite blend of two or three cheeses from one country. In this recipe Swiss cheeses are used.

1 garlic clove, halved
450 ml (¾ pint) dry white wine
250 g (8 oz) Emmental cheese, grated
250 g (8 oz) Gruyère cheese, grated
250 g (8 oz) Royalpe cheese, grated

1 tablespoon cornflour
2 tablespoons kirsch or vodka
a pinch of ground nutmeg
black pepper

1 Rub the cut side of the garlic around the inside of the fondue pan. Pour in the wine and bring to the boil on the hob.
2 Reduce the heat. Gradually add the grated cheeses, a little at a time, stirring constantly until they have melted.
3 Blend the cornflour with the kirsch or vodka, and stir into the fondue. Cook, stirring constantly, until the mixture is thick and creamy. Stir in the nutmeg and pepper to taste.
4 Transfer the fondue pan to its lighted spirit stove to keep warm.

FOR DIPPING

Offer cubes of toasted french bread, Herb Croustades (page 121), cooked pizza, cubes of Granary bread and Parsley Biscuits (page 115). Sticks of crisp celery, wedges of tomato and apples are also delicious.
Pictured on the front cover

SOMERSET FONDUE

SERVES 4–6

This fondue can be a little sweet in flavour, so slightly tart dessert apples go particularly well with it.

½ small onion
300 ml (½ pint) dry cider or apple juice
1 teaspoon lemon juice
500 g (1 lb) farmhouse Cheddar cheese, grated

4 teaspoons cornflour
2 tablespoons sherry (optional) or water
a pinch of dry mustard
a few drops of Tabasco sauce

1 Rub the onion around the inside of the fondue pan. Add the cider or apple juice and the lemon juice, bring to the boil on the hob, then reduce the heat to a simmer.
2 Gradually add the cheese, stirring constantly until melted.
3 Blend the cornflour with the sherry (if using) or water, the mustard and Tabasco sauce. Stir into the fondue and cook for a further 2 minutes until the mixture is thick and creamy.
4 Carefully transfer the fondue pan to the lighted spirit stove, to serve.

FOR DIPPING

Choose crisp dessert apples and pears and allow one fruit, cored and cut into chunks, per person. Cooked pork chipolatas, cubes of cured ham and cooked celeriac or parsnip offer a savoury alternative.

TUNA AND SWEETCORN FONDUE

SERVES 6

125 g (4 oz) butter
1 large onion, chopped finely
375 g (12 oz) Cheddar cheese, grated
4 tablespoons single cream
1 tablespoon Worcestershire sauce
2 tablespoons tomato purée
200 g (7 oz) can of tuna in brine

200 g (7 oz) can of sweetcorn kernels, drained
salt and pepper
1 tablespoon finely chopped fresh parsley

1 Melt the butter in the fondue pan on the hob, and cook the onion until soft and golden.
2 Gradually add the cheese, cream, Worcestershire sauce, tomato purée and the brine from the drained tuna fish.

3 Cook very gently, stirring constantly, until the cheese has melted and the sauce is smooth.
4 Add the tuna fish and sweetcorn kernels. Season to taste, with a little salt and pepper. Sprinkle in the chopped parsley.
5 Transfer the fondue pan to its lighted spirit stove to keep warm.

———————— FOR DIPPING ————————

Offer chunks of cooked potato, raw button mushrooms and squares of green or red pepper.
French bread, Curried Bread Cubes (page 121), crispy fried potato skins, and Parsley Biscuits (page 115) also go well with this.

PLOUGHMAN'S FONDUE

———————— SERVES 4 ————————

1 garlic clove, halved
450 ml (¾ pint) light ale
375 g (12 oz) Cheddar or double Gloucester cheese, grated

25 g (1 oz) butter
1 teaspoon dry mustard
2 tablespoons cornflour

1 Rub the cut side of the garlic clove around the inside of the fondue pan.
2 Pour in the beer and heat on the hob until just bubbling. Gradually add the cheese, stirring until melted. Stir in the butter.
3 Blend the mustard and cornflour with a little water and stir into the fondue. Continue to cook over a gentle heat until it thickens.
4 Transfer the fondue pan to its lighted spirit stove to keep warm.

———————— FOR DIPPING ————————

As the name implies, this fondue should be served with chunks of crusty white or Granary bread, pieces of celery, pickled onions, gherkins, cherry tomatoes and wedges of crisp dessert apple.

Ploughman's Fondue (page 17)

CHEESE FONDUE à la BRILLAT SAVARIN

'Weigh the number of eggs which you want to use. This depends on how many people are going to eat with you. Take a piece of good Gruyère weighing a third and butter weighing a sixth of the weight of the eggs. Break the eggs and beat them well in a casserole. Add the butter and the cheese, grated and minced. Put the casserole on a hot stove and stir with a wooden spoon until the mixture is suitably thickened and is smooth. Add a very little or hardly any salt, depending on the age of the cheese. Add a good portion of pepper, which is one of the distinguishing characters of this ancient dish. Serve on a lightly heated dish.'

CRUNCHY BACON AND EGGS FONDUE

———— SERVES 4–5 ————

This is a version of the gastronome Brillat-Savarin's original cheese fondue recipe. It is more like a creamy scrambled egg than a cheese fondue in the Swiss sense, and the addition of crisp bacon makes it an ideal 'brunch'. Hence, its modern name. The fondue must be cooked very slowly to give a smooth texture.

75 g (3 oz) streaky bacon rashers, de-rinded and chopped
6 eggs, beaten
125 g (4 oz) butter, cut into pieces

125 g (4 oz) Gruyère cheese, grated
50 g (2 oz) Sbrinz or parmesan cheese, freshly grated
salt and pepper

1 Fry the bacon in its own fat in the fondue pan on the hob until crisp and well browned. Drain the bacon bits and transfer them to a plate.
2 Tip the beaten eggs into the fondue pan, add half the butter and heat very gently, stirring, for 2 minutes.
3 Add the remaining butter and continue to stir constantly over a low heat until the butter has melted.
4 Take the fondue pan off the heat and stir in the two cheeses. Beat well with a wooden spoon, to combine all the ingredients.
5 Transfer the fondue pan to its lighted spirit stove and continue to cook very gently, stirring frequently, until the mixture thickens.
6 Stir in the crisp bacon bits, and season well with salt and pepper.

———— FOR DIPPING ————

This rich fondue is best eaten with crusty bread or crumpet cubes. Allow 175–250 g (6–8 oz) per person. The fondue can be spooned into warmed individual bowls and eaten with a fork, if preferred.

WELSH RABBIT

───── *MAKES 4 SLICES* ─────

This dish is similar to the cheese fondue and has equally entertaining stories about its origin! Welsh wives, spying husbands or sons returning from a hunt empty-handed, would protest by setting pots of cheese to melt before the fire as a substitute for a dinner of game. The fondue pan is perfect for melting the cheese – and it's a nice story to tell while stirring the fondue!

15 g (½ oz) butter
3 tablespoons brown ale
250 g (8 oz) Cheddar cheese, grated
1 teaspoon dry mustard

a dash of Tabasco sauce
4 large slices of lightly toasted bread
fresh parsley sprigs to garnish

1 Melt the butter in the fondue pan. Add the ale and the cheese and heat very gently until the cheese has melted.
2 Stir in the mustard and the Tabasco sauce.
3 Divide the mixture between the slices of toast. Place the slices under a preheated grill and cook for 1–2 minutes until golden and bubbling.
4 Garnish each slice with a sprig of parsley. Serve immediately, accompanied by sweet pickle and tomato wedges. For a more substantial supper dish, top the cheese mixture with a poached egg and make a Golden Buck!

QUICK TOMATO FONDUE

───── *SERVES 4* ─────

375 g (12 oz) mature Cheddar cheese,
grated
175 g (6 oz) Gouda cheese, grated
300 ml (½ pint) condensed tomato soup

3 tablespoons tomato purée
3 tablespoons sherry
2 teaspoons Worcestershire sauce
salt and pepper

1 Combine all the ingredients in the fondue pan. Place on the hob over a low heat and stir constantly until the cheese has melted. Season to taste.
2 Transfer the fondue pan to its lighted spirit stove to keep warm.

───── *FOR DIPPING* ─────

Buy an assortment of sliced salamis, ham and frankfurters. Roll up slices of salami and ham onto cocktail sticks or forks. Allow 50–75 g (2–3 oz) per person. Chunks of french bread, Peanut Cookies (page 117), cooked pizza, Curried Bread Cubes (page 121), gherkins and olives will complement the meats and fondue.

DEVILLED CHESHIRE FONDUE

SERVES 5–6

25 g (1 oz) butter
2 tablespoons plain flour
450 ml (¾ pint) milk
375 g (12 oz) mild Cheshire cheese,
grated

2 teapoons Worcestershire sauce
1 teaspoon cream of horseradish sauce
½ teaspoon salt
1 teaspoon mild paprika pepper
2 tablespoons medium dry sherry

1 Melt the butter in the fondue pan on the hob. Sprinkle in the flour and cook, stirring constantly, for 1 minute.
2 Gradually blend in the milk, stirring, until the sauce is smooth and thickened.
3 Add the cheese, Worcestershire sauce, horseradish sauce, salt, paprika pepper and sherry. Continue stirring until the fondue is creamy.
4 Transfer the fondue pan to its lighted spirit stove to keep warm.

FOR DIPPING

Offer cubes of french bread, bread sticks, Peanut Cookies (page 117), muffin cubes or Parsley Biscuits (page 115).
Wedges of avocado pear dipped in lemon juice and an assorted platter of vegetable crudités – carrots, cauliflower florets, button mushrooms, celery, etc. – will also go very well with this fondue.

HERRINGS IN OATMEAL WITH MUSTARD DIP

SERVES 4–6

No matter how carefully herrings are prepared, there are always very fine bones left in them. However, they are worth eating to enjoy this traditional Scottish recipe – fondue style.

8 herring fillets
3 tablespoons seasoned flour
1 teaspoon dry mustard
2 eggs, beaten
125 g (4 oz) fine oatmeal
600 ml (1 pint) oil for frying

MUSTARD AND DILL DIP
½ quantity of Basic Mayonnaise
(page 104)
2 tablespoons Dijon mustard
2 tablespoons chopped fresh or
1 teaspoon dried dill
1 tablespoon white wine vinegar
3 tablespoons single cream

1 Cut the herring fillets into strips 1 cm (½ inch) wide. Place in a polythene bag with the seasoned flour and mustard and toss thoroughly to coat the fish in the flour.
2 Dip the herring into the beaten egg and then into the oatmeal to coat completely. Place on a serving plate and refrigerate until required.
3 Prepare the mustard and dill dip: combine all the ingredients in a small bowl. Cover and chill until required.
4 Heat the oil in the fondue pan. Carefully transfer the fondue pan to its lighted spirit stove to keep hot.
5 Individually cook the strips of herring in oatmeal until golden brown. Then transfer to an eating fork, dip into the sauce and serve accompanied by jacket potatoes, and cucumber or green bean and tomato salad.

CREAMY MUSHROOM FONDUE

———— SERVES 4–5 ————

75 g (3 oz) butter
1 medium-size onion, chopped finely
2 garlic cloves, chopped finely
375 g (12 oz) button mushrooms,
chopped
3 tablespoons plain flour

450 ml (¾ pint) milk
125 g (4 oz) Gruyère cheese, grated
4 tablespoons double cream
4 tablespoons dry sherry (optional)
2 tablespoons freshly chopped parsley
salt and pepper

1 Melt the butter in the fondue pan on the hob and cook the onion, garlic and mushrooms for 10 minutes until softened.
2 Sprinkle on the flour and cook for a further minute, stirring. Remove the pan from the heat and gradually blend in the milk until smooth. Return the pan to the heat and bring to the boil, stirring constantly until the sauce has thickened.
3 Remove the pan from the heat and add the cheese, cream, sherry (if using), parsley and salt and pepper to taste. Stir until the cheese has melted.
4 Transfer the fondue pan to the lighted spirit stove to keep warm.

———— FOR DIPPING ————

Savoury Choux Puffs (page 120), Herb Croustades (page 121), Gruyère Moons (page 116), deep-fried potato skins and cooked chipolata sausages will go well with this fondue; or simply serve french bread, cubes of cooked chicken and ham, and a three-bean salad or an avocado and tomato salad.

FISH AND POTATO NUGGETS

SERVES 4–6

These nuggets are a smaller version of a fishcake. Chill the nuggets thoroughly before frying so they are really firm to skewer.

375 g (12 oz) cooked, flaked white fish
(e.g. cod, coley or whiting)
500 g (1 lb) mashed potato
2 tablespoons chopped fresh parsley

2 eggs, beaten
125 g (4 oz) dry breadcrumbs
600 ml (1 pint) oil for frying
salt and pepper

1 Fork the flaked fish into the mashed potato. Stir in the chopped parsley, and add salt and pepper to taste. Chill for approximately 1 hour. The consistency needs to be fairly dry and firm.
2 Roll small spoonfuls of the mixture between the palms of your hands or on a lightly floured board, to make 20–24 small balls.
3 Coat the balls in the beaten egg and then in the breadcrumbs. Chill for a further 30 minutes, or until required.
4 Heat the oil in the fondue pan. Carefully transfer the pan to its lighted spirit stove to keep hot.
5 Fry the nuggets until golden and crisp.

COOK'S HINT

To make a change from breadcrumbs, make up a crispy crumb coating. Mix together dry breadcrumbs, sesame seeds and finely chopped almonds or peanuts or parmesan cheese. Crushed potato crisps and commercially prepared stuffing mixes (e.g. lemon and parsley) work well too.

FOR DIPPING

Serve these crispy nuggets with a choice of two or three sauces from the following: Spicy Tomato Dip (page 111), Sour Cream and Chive Dip (page 107), Tartare Sauce (page 105), Sweet Red Pepper Sauce (page 113), Quick Béarnaise Sauce (page 110), Tomato Mayonnaise (page 106).

TROPICAL GAMMON WITH PINEAPPLE

SERVES 4

Try apricot halves instead of pineapple cubes for a change. Although the apricot juice will not have the same meat-tenderising effect that pineapple juice does, it is still very good.

500 g (1 lb) gammon steak or
gammon rashers
475 g (15 oz) can of pineapple chunks
in own juice
1 small onion, diced finely
4 tablespoons white wine vinegar

4 tablespoons redcurrant jelly
2 teaspoons dry mustard
1 tablespoon light soft brown sugar
2 teaspoons cornflour
2 kiwifruit, peeled
600 ml (1 pint) oil for frying

1 Cut the gammon steaks or rashers into strips 5 × 1 cm (2 × ½ inch). Place in a bowl.

2 Drain the pineapple chunks and put to one side. Reserve 6 tablespoons of the juice and pour the remainder over the gammon. Stir in the chopped onion. Cover and marinate for 1 hour.

3 Meanwhile, make up the sauce. In a small saucepan, gently heat the white wine vinegar, redcurrant jelly, mustard powder and sugar, stirring until the jelly has dissolved.

4 Blend the cornflour with the reserved pineapple juice and add to the sauce, stirring until slightly thickened. Reduce the heat and gently simmer the sauce.

5 Drain the gammon strips and pat dry with a piece of kitchen paper towel. Divide between four serving plates.

6 Cut the kiwifruit into quarters and then into half again. Divide between four plates, together with the pineapple cubes.

7 Heat the oil in the fondue pan, then carefully transfer the pan to its lighted stove to keep hot.

8 Skewer a piece of gammon steak onto a fondue fork and cook in the oil for 3 minutes or until tender. Transfer the meat on to a dinner fork and skewer on a piece of kiwifruit or pineapple.

9 Pour the warm sauce into a bowl. Dip the meat and fruit into the warm sauce. Serve this fondue accompanied by boiled rice.

Tropical Gammon with Pineapple (page 25)

SAUSAGE FONDUE

SERVES 6–8

These tasty sausage parcels can be prepared well in advance and then served as part of a fondue meal.

12 large sausages, cooked
12–15 streaky bacon rashers, de-rinded

150 g (5 oz) Edam or mozzarella cheese
600 ml (1 pint) oil for frying

1 Cut each sausage into three equal-sized pieces and then partially cut each piece along its length to form a pocket.
2 Using the back of a knife, stretch the bacon rashers on a board. Cut each rasher into 3 equal lengths.
3 Slice the cheese into 36 pieces, to tuck inside the sausage pieces.
4 Make up the parcels. Place a piece of cheese inside each sausage, then tightly wrap a piece of bacon around the sausage. Secure with a cocktail stick and chill.
5 Heat the oil in the fondue pan and then carefully transfer the pan to its lighted spirit stove to keep hot.
6 Skewer a sausage parcel onto the fondue fork and cook in the oil for 2–3 minutes or until the bacon is crisp. Transfer to an eating fork and serve with pickles or chutney, crusty bread, or one of the following dips.

FOR DIPPING

Spicy Tomato Dip (page 111), Tomato Mayonnaise (page 106), Sweet and Sour Barbecue Sauce (page 112), Garlic Dip (page 107), Mild Curry Sauce (page 109).

SHEPHERD'S FONDUE WITH MEATBALLS

SERVES 5–6

375 g (12 oz) minced lamb
40 g (1½ oz) fresh white breadcrumbs
1 garlic clove, chopped finely
1 shallot, chopped finely
a little flour for dusting

2 tablespoons vegetable oil
1 quantity of Somerset Fondue (page 16)
2 tablespoons chopped fresh chives
750 g (1½ lb) cooked potato, cut into chunks
salt and pepper

1 First make the meatballs: place the lamb, breadcrumbs, garlic and shallot in a food processor and blend them until smooth. Alternatively mix them thoroughly by hand.

2 Divide the mixture into 24–26 equal portions and roll into 2.5 cm (1-inch) balls. Lightly dust them in some flour.
3 Heat the oil in a non-stick frying pan and cook the meatballs for 10–15 minutes until brown. Transfer to a serving dish to keep warm with the potatoes.
4 Prepare the Somerset Fondue. Stir in the chives. Transfer the fondue pan to its lighted spirit stove to keep warm.
5 Divide the warm meatballs and potato between 5–6 serving plates for dipping into the fondue.

REFRIGERATOR CHOCOLATE FONDUE

—————— SERVES 6–8 ——————

This economical chocolate fondue is a great stand-by. Once made it can be kept in the refrigerator for a couple of weeks and gently reheated when required, or poured straight over fruit and ice cream as an instant sauce.

400 g (13 oz) can of evaporated milk
175 g (6 oz) granulated sugar
75 g (3 oz) plain cooking chocolate,
broken into pieces

2 teaspoons cocoa powder
1½ tablespoons cornflour
a few drops of vanilla essence
1 tablespoon brandy or rum (optional)

1 Gently heat the evaporated milk, sugar and chocolate in the fondue pan until the sugar has dissolved and the chocolate has melted.
2 Blend together the cocoa powder, cornflour and vanilla essence with the brandy or rum, if using, or a tablespoon of cold water.
3 Stir this into the fondue pan, increase the heat slightly and cook, stirring, until the sauce thickens.
4 Transfer the fondue pan to its lighted spirit stove to keep warm over a low flame.

—————— FOR DIPPING ——————

Serve some coconut ice, flapjack, baby Sweet Choux Puffs (page 120) filled with whipped cream, or wedges of commercially prepared arctic roll. Drained canned pears and apricots also go well with this fondue.

HONEY AND GREEK YOGURT FONDUE

———————— SERVES 4–5 ————————

Do make sure the yogurt does not boil – it just needs to be warmed through very gently.

300 ml (½ pint) thick Greek yogurt
2–3 tablespoons clear honey

grated rind and juice of ½ orange
a pinch of ground cinnamon

1 Mix together the yogurt, honey and grated orange rind and juice. Pour into the chocolate fondue pan and heat the yogurt through very gently, until lukewarm.
2 Transfer the fondue pan to its lighted candle to keep warm.
3 Just before serving, sprinkle the cinnamon over the surface.

———————— FOR DIPPING ————————

Offer a selection of dried fruit (the pre-soaked variety is best). Allow approximately 75 g (3 oz) per person, to include apricots, pears, prunes, apple rings and peaches.
Fresh bananas, grapes and figs will also go well – allow 1 piece of fruit per person.
Serve with crisp shortbread fingers, Peanut Cookies (page 117) or wafer biscuits.

FONDUES
for
FRIENDS

SWISS CHEESE FONDUE

(FONDUE NEUCHÂTEL) SERVES 4–6

Fondue is the national dish of Switzerland, with each region having its own variation, customs and, of course, special cheeses. Fondue Neuchâtel traditionally has equal amounts of Emmental and Gruyère, but the following proportions will give you a less 'stringy' result when dipping in the bread.

1 garlic clove, halved
300 ml (½ pint) dry white wine
1 teaspoon lemon juice
425 g (14 oz) Gruyère cheese, grated coarsely

200 g (7 oz) Emmental cheese, grated coarsely
1 tablespoon cornflour
3 tablespoons kirsch, gin or vodka
a pinch of grated nutmeg
a pinch of white pepper

1 Rub the garlic around the inside of the fondue pan. Add the wine and lemon juice, and bring to the boil, then reduce the heat to a simmer.
2 Gradually add the cheeses, stirring constantly until melted.
3 Blend the cornflour with the kirsch, gin or vodka and stir into the fondue. Cook for 2 minutes until the sauce thickens slightly.
4 Season to taste, with nutmeg and white pepper.
5 Carefully transfer the fondue pan to the lighted spirit stove, to serve.

FOR DIPPING

Allow 175–250 g (6–8 oz) crusty french bread, cut into thick slices and quartered, per person. This ensures a piece of crust on each cube, making it easier to skewer on to the fork. Hard-boiled quail eggs and chunks of dessert apple and pear taste delicious, too – allow 900 g (2 lb) prepared fruit for 6 servings.

ROSÉ FONDUE

SERVES 4

This fondue was supposedly discovered when a group of skiers, stranded over-night in a chalet in the mountains, made a traditional Swiss cheese fondue with a dry rosé wine (in the absence of a dry white wine) – it was delicious and quite distinctive in flavour, and colour. It has since become well known in Switzerland. A pink fondue could be made using Red Windsor cheese instead of or as well as the rosé wine.

SUMMER GREEN FONDUE

SERVES 4–6

This is just the recipe to cope with a glut of courgettes, and it is ideal for using up frozen courgettes too.

500 g (1 lb) courgettes, sliced
1 large onion, chopped finely
150 ml (¼ pint) vegetable stock
150 ml (¼ pint) medium white wine
250 g (8 oz) roulé cheese with herbs,
diced
2 teaspoons cornflour

2 tablespoons water
125 ml (4 fl oz) single cream
1 tablespoon finely chopped fresh
chervil
1 tablespoon finely chopped fresh
chives
salt and pepper

1 In a large pan, simmer the courgettes and onion with the stock and wine for approximately 20 minutes or until tender. Sieve or purée the mixture and transfer to the fondue pan.
2 Bring the courgette mixture to a steady simmer and then gradually stir in cubes of cheese, until blended.
3 Mix the cornflour with the water and stir into the fondue. Continue to heat gently, stirring, until the mixture thickens slightly. Season to taste with salt and pepper.
4 Transfer the fondue pan to its lighted spirit stove to keep warm. Stir in the cream and fresh herbs. Do not allow the fondue to boil.

FOR DIPPING

Offer a selection of thinly sliced salamis, hams and sausages, rolled up on to the fondue forks, cubes of ham and crispy bacon rolls, allowing 125 g (4 oz) per person.
Serve with cubes of pumpernickel, french or Granary bread, Herb Croustades (page 121) or an Italian bread like ciabatta.

FRENCH BRIE AND ONION FONDUE

SERVES 5–6

Try making this fondue with one of the speciality Bries now available: there are mushroom, black pepper and herb varieties to choose from. Boursin cheese will also work well.

50 g (2 oz) butter
2 medium-size onions, chopped finely
25 g (1 oz) plain flour
300 ml (½ pint) chicken stock

375 g (12 oz) ripe French Brie
150 ml (¼ pint) double cream
2 tablespoons fresh chopped parsley
salt and pepper

1 Melt the butter in the fondue pan on the hob and cook the onions gently for 10–15 minutes until softened and light golden.
2 Sprinkle on the flour, and continue cooking for 1–2 minutes, stirring to blend in the flour.
3 Gradually blend in the chicken stock, stirring, until the mixture thickens. Simmer for 4–5 minutes.
4 Meanwhile, cut away the rind and slice the cheese thinly. Stir into the fondue, together with the cream. Cook gently, stirring occasionally, until the mixture is smooth.
5 Stir in the parsley and season to taste with salt and pepper.
6 Transfer the fondue pan to its lighted spirit stove to keep warm.

FOR DIPPING

Enjoy this fondue with pieces of french bread, Garlic Bread Cubes (page 121) and Parsley Biscuits (page 115). Raw button mushrooms would also go well; allow 50 g (2 oz) per person.

AVOCADO AND WENSLEYDALE CHEESE FONDUE

──────── *SERVES 6* ────────

It is essential to use ripe avocados for this recipe, and the secret of creating a beautiful green colour is to scrape the inside of the avocado skins with a spoon to remove all the creamy dark green layer which adds so much flavour and colour to any avocado dish.

25 g (1 oz) butter
1 small onion, chopped finely
2 large ripe avocados, halved and stoned
2 tablespoons lemon juice
200 ml (½ pint) dry white wine
175 g (6 oz) Wensleydale cheese, crumbled

15 g (½ oz) fresh parmesan cheese, grated
6 tablespoons single cream
1 tablespoon cornflour
a dash of Tabasco
salt and pepper

1 Melt the butter in the fondue pan on the hob and cook the onion for 5 minutes until softened but not coloured.
2 Mash or purée the avocado flesh with the lemon juice until smooth.
3 Heat the wine in the fondue pan, then gradually add the cheeses. Cook gently, stirring occasionally, until the cheese melts.
4 Stir in the puréed avocado, the cream blended with the cornflour, a dash of Tabasco and salt and pepper to taste. Continue stirring over a low heat until the fondue is smooth and creamy.
5 Transfer the fondue pan to its lighted spirit stove to keep warm.

──────── *FOR DIPPING* ────────

For special occasions or as part of a buffet or cocktails, serve a platter of crudités: raw, crisp carrot, red pepper and celery sticks, cauliflower florets, radishes, baby tomatoes, spring onions, and button mushrooms. As a main course, serve with the above plus cooked bacon rolls, peeled prawns, Savoury Choux Puffs (page 120) and Garlic Bread Cubes (page 121).

Avocado and Wensleydale Cheese Fondue, with Savoury Choux Puffs (page 120) and
Garlic Bread Cubes (page 121)

HAWAIIAN FONDUE

SERVES 6

375 ml (12 fl oz) white wine such as
frascati or a sparkling wine,
or white grape juice
375 g (12 oz) Gruyère cheese, grated
75 g (3 oz) cream cheese (such as
Philadelphia), cubed
2 tablespoons cornflour

2 tablespoons lemon juice
½ teaspoon ground ginger
1 tablespoon white rum (optional)
1 fresh pineapple
500–750 g (1–1½ lb) piece of cooked
ham, cubed
salt and pepper

1 Heat the wine or grape juice in the fondue pan on the hob, then gradually
add the Gruyère cheese and cream cheese. Stir until the cheeses have
melted.
2 Blend the cornflour with the lemon juice and add to the fondue with the
ground ginger. Stir constantly over a gentle heat until the mixture is
smooth and creamy.
3 Stir in the rum (if using). Season to taste with salt and pepper.
4 Transfer the fondue pan to its lighted spirit stove to keep warm.
5 Halve the pineapple lengthways and remove the flesh. Cut the flesh into
bite-sized cubes. Mix the pineapple and ham together and spoon them back
into the pineapple shells for serving.

Accompany with crusty french bread or a lightly curried rice or pasta salad.

SALMON AND DOUBLE GLOUCESTER FONDUE

MAKES 4 SLICES

15 g (½ oz) butter
2 spring onions, chopped finely
3 tablespoons milk
250 g (8 oz) double Gloucester cheese,
grated
1 teaspoon Worcestershire sauce

½ teaspoon dry mustard
75 g (3 oz) can of red salmon, drained
and flaked
4 large slices of lightly toasted bread
salt and pepper

1 Melt the butter in the fondue pan, add the spring onions and cook gently for
a minute.
2 Add the milk, cheese, Worcestershire sauce, mustard and salt and pepper to
taste.
3 Stir over a gentle heat until the cheese has melted. Stir in the red salmon.
4 Divide the fondue mixture between the slices of toast. Place the slices
under a preheated grill and cook for 1–2 minutes until golden and
bubbling. Serve immediately.

IRISH CHEESE FONDUE WITH SODA BREAD

——— SERVES 6 ———

This could be one for the men! It is quite strong, but pleasant – and a tot of whiskey should accompany the fondue midway.

1 garlic clove, halved
200 ml (7 fl oz) dry white wine
500 g (1 lb) mature Irish Cheddar cheese, grated

1 tablespoon cornflour
3 tablespoons Irish whiskey
a pinch of white pepper

1 Rub the inside of the fondue pan with the cut side of the garlic clove. Pour in the wine, and heat gently.
2 Gradually add the cheese to the warm wine, stirring with a wooden spoon, until the cheese has melted.
3 Blend the cornflour with the whiskey, and add this to the fondue, stirring until the mixture thickens. Add white pepper, to taste.
4 Transfer the fondue pan to its lighted spirit stove to keep warm.

——— FOR DIPPING ———

Buy or make (page 122) some soda bread; it can be quite dense, but is perfect for dipping into a fondue.
Commercially prepared potato cakes, toasted and cut into bite-size pieces, or 'baby' new potatoes will also go well.

SCOTCH RAREBIT

—————— SERVES 4–5 ——————

A variation of the Welsh Rabbit – and with a different story about its origin! Apparently the 'rabbit' is called 'rarebit' because, once upon a time hors d'oeuvre were known as 'forebits' – as they were served before a meal. The characteristic cheese savouries that came at the end of a meal were, therefore, called 'rarebits'.

50 g (2 oz) butter
250 ml (8 fl oz) stout or beer
275 g (9 oz) white Stilton cheese,
crumbled

75 g (3 oz) Cheshire cheese, crumbled
1 teaspoon dry mustard
a pinch of ground white pepper
6 slices of hot buttered toast

1 Heat the butter and stout together in the fondue pan until just simmering.
2 Add the crumbled cheese, a little at a time, stirring until the cheese has melted.
3 Add the mustard and white pepper.
4 Transfer the fondue pan to its lighted spirit stove to keep warm over a low flame.

—————— FOR DIPPING/SERVING ——————

Cut the buttered toast into small triangles and place in bowls. Ladle the fondue over the toast. Alternatively, use the toast for dipping.
Accompany with wedges of ripe pear and some crisp celery or use them for dipping.

HOT HERB DIP WITH POTATOES

—————— SERVES 6–8 ——————

This recipe from the eastern part of Switzerland would originally have been cooked in an old earthenware *caquelon*. It is also known as *stupfete* which means 'to dip in', though, because of its runny consistency it is best served with potatoes and as an accompaniment to roast meats – particularly lamb and beef.

1 kg (2 lb) new potatoes
6 tablespoons vegetable oil
500 g (1 lb) onions, chopped finely
25 g (1 oz) fresh parsley, chopped
finely

15 g (½ oz) fresh chives, chopped
finely
1 teaspoon salt
½ teaspoon ground black pepper
125 ml (4 fl oz) dry white wine
2 tablespoons white wine vinegar

1 Boil the potatoes in their skins until just tender. Keep warm.
2 Heat the oil in the fondue pan and fry the onions for 5 minutes until softened.
3 Stir in the parsley, chives, salt, pepper, wine and vinegar. Simmer for a further 5 minutes.
4 Carefully transfer the fondue pan to its lighted spirit stove to keep warm.

——————— FOR DIPPING ———————

Serve the dip with the new potatoes and ladled over hot or cold roast meats. Have some crusty bread to mop up the juices.

FONDUE BOURGUIGNONNE

——————— SERVES 4–5 ———————

This is the traditional meat fondue using good quality steak. However, mixed meat fondues are also popular. Small sausages, bacon rolls, pork, chicken and liver can be included – but do make sure they are cooked through thoroughly. The meat and sauces can be prepared a day in advance, and can be served with jacket potatoes, french bread and salads.

1 kg (2 lb) fillet of beef	*1 bay leaf*
600 ml (1 pint) oil for frying	*1 garlic clove*

1 Prepare the meat; trim away any fat and cut into 2.5 cm (1-inch) cubes. Dry the meat on kitchen paper and divide between four or five small dishes.
2 Heat the oil in the fondue pot to the correct temperature of 190°C/375°F. Test by dropping a small cube of bread into the oil – it should turn brown in less than a minute. If the oil is too hot and smoking, allow it to cool slightly.
3 Carefully transfer the fondue pan to its lighted spirit stove to keep hot. Drop in the bay leaf and garlic, for extra flavouring.
4 Each person cooks the cubes of meat in the oil until done to the individual's taste.
5 Transfer the meat from the fondue fork onto an eating fork and dip into a sauce.

——————— FOR DIPPING ———————

Offer a selection of 3 or 4 sauces to dip the meat in chosen from the following: Quick Béarnaise Sauce (page 110), Cumberland Sauce (page 111), Mild Curry Sauce (page 109), Pesto Sauce (page 109), Garlic Dip (page 107), Red Pepper Sauce with Chilli (page 113), Spicy Tomato Dip (page 111), as well as a choice of mustards and relishes.

SPICY TOMATO FONDUE

SERVES 6–8

This is a perfect accompaniment to barbecued meats – sausages, chicken drumsticks and sizzling spare ribs. To cater for the English weather, it may be worthwhile making this in advance and freezing it. It can then be reheated for that impromptu occasion!

4 tablespoons vegetable oil
1 garlic clove, chopped finely
1 medium-size onion, chopped finely
1 celery stick, chopped
1 small carrot, diced
2 × 425 g (14 oz) cans chopped tomatoes
1 green pepper, de-seeded and diced
2 teaspoons tomato purée

1 tablespoon red wine vinegar
1 tablespoon Worcestershire sauce
1 rounded tablespoon soft light brown sugar
2 teaspoons chopped fresh basil, (or ½ teaspoon dried basil)
2 teaspoons snipped fresh chives
salt and pepper

1 Heat the oil in the fondue pan. Cook the garlic and onion gently until softened. Add the celery and carrot and cook for a further 5 minutes.
2 Add the remaining ingredients with the exceptions of the fresh herbs. Stir in a little salt and pepper. Simmer, covered, for 30 minutes. Cool slightly.
3 Purée the sauce in an electric blender or food processor and then sieve the sauce into the fondue pan.
4 Check and adjust the seasoning, if necessary. Stir in the herbs.
5 Transfer the fondue pan to its lighted spirit stove to keep warm over a low flame.

FOR DIPPING

Serve warm with grilled meats – chicken drumsticks, hamburgers, sausages, kebabs.
Pieces of baked jacket potatoes, pizza squares, barbecued sweetcorn and barbecued onions will also be delicious dipped into this fondue. Also offer cubes of cheese, garlic bread and bread sticks.

COOK'S HINT

Do not purée or sieve the sauce if you prefer it chunky. Any leftovers can be served with a portion of freshly cooked pasta.

BARBECUED FRUIT KEBABS WITH CALYPSO FONDUE

SERVES 8

This dessert makes a delicious ending to a barbecue and requires little preparation. Of course, if the weather is not up to it, you can cook the kebabs under a conventional grill!

KEBABS	FONDUE
1 large apple, cored	*300 ml (½ pint) double cream*
2 kiwifruit, quartered	*50 g (2 oz) creamed coconut, cubed*
2 peaches, quartered	*1 tablespoon caster sugar*
16 firm strawberries	*1 tablespoon cornflour*
16 pineapple chunks, fresh or canned	*2 tablespoons white rum or the juice of*
2 small bananas, cut into four	*1 orange*
juice of ½ lemon	*grated nutmeg*
125 g (4 oz) butter	
2 tablespoons clear honey	
finely grated rind of 1 orange	

1 First make the kebabs. Quarter the apple and then cut each wedge in half across the middle. Dip the apple and banana pieces into lemon juice.
2 Divide and thread the fruits onto 8 metal skewers.
3 Melt the butter in a small saucepan on the side of the barbecue; stir in the honey and orange rind.
4 Meanwhile, prepare the fondue. Heat the cream in the chocolate fondue pan together with the creamed coconut and the caster sugar. Stir frequently.
5 When the ingredients have dissolved, blend the cornflour and rum or orange juice together and stir it into the cream. Continue to stir over a gentle heat until the fondue thickens.
6 Grate a little nutmeg over the surface of the fondue and transfer the pan onto its stand above the lighted candle to keep warm.
7 Lay the fruit kebabs on the barbecue grid, approximately 15 cm (6 inches) above the glowing coals. Brush liberally with the melted butter mixture and cook for 5–7 minutes, basting and turning frequently to brown evenly.
8 Serve the kebabs with the warm coconut calypso fondue. Each guest can remove the barbecued fruits from the skewers and dip them into the fondue.

FOR DIPPING

Also serve Coconut Macaroons (page 123) and sponge cake with the fruit kebabs.

*Barbecued Fruit Kebabs with Calypso Fondue (page 41), with Coconut Macaroons
(page 123)*

SWISS TOBLERONE FONDUE

SERVES 6

Choose your favourite variety of Toblerone to make this truly authentic chocolate fondue.

375 g (12 oz) Toblerone chocolate
150 ml (¼ pint) double cream

2 tablespoons kirsch or amaretto
liqueur

1 Break the chocolate bar into pieces and place in the chocolate fondue pan with the cream.
2 Place over a very low heat and stir frequently until the chocolate melts. Stir in the kirsch or amaretto liqueur.
3 Transfer the fondue pan onto its stand above the lighted candle flame, to keep warm.

FOR DIPPING

Have ready bowls of chilled fresh strawberries, raspberries and cherries. Allow 175 g (6 oz) fruit for each person.
Ratafia biscuits and sponge fingers also go well: allow 25–50 g (1–2 oz) per person. Or offer Schenkeli (page 116) or marzipan.

CHRISTMAS FRUIT FONDUE

SERVES 6

12 dried apricots
6 prunes
6 dates
4 tablespoons brandy or rum
1 quantity of Bitter Chocolate and

Orange Fondue (page 93)
50 g (2 oz) walnuts or brazil nuts
6 pieces crystallised pineapple
2 satsumas, divided into segments
2 Cox's apples, cored and cubed

1 Marinate the apricots, prunes and dates in the brandy or rum for 1 hour.
2 Prepare the Bitter Chocolate and Orange Fondue.
3 Divide the marinated fruits, nuts and crystallised and fresh fruits between 6 individual dessert plates and serve with the chocolate fondue.

FOR DIPPING

As well as the Christmas fruits, offer commercially prepared or home-made brandy snaps and spiced biscuits with the fondue.

FONDUES
for the
YOUNG SET

BANGERS 'N' BEANS FONDUE

Always a firm favourite with children (and adults!), baked beans will add a 'wild west' flavour to a fondue supper for the tribe.

1 tablespoon vegetable oil
1 smoked bacon rasher, de-rinded and chopped
425 g (14 oz) can baked beans
150 ml (¼ pint) tomato ketchup

1 teaspoon black treacle
2 teaspoons cornflour
½ teaspoon dry mustard
4 tablespoons water

1 Heat the oil in the fondue pan on the hob and fry the bacon until crisp and golden brown.
2 Stir in the baked beans, tomato ketchup and the treacle. Bring to a steady boil.
3 Blend together the cornflour and mustard with the water and stir into the fondue. Stir constantly until the fondue thickens slightly.
4 Transfer the fondue pan to its lighted spirit stove to keep warm.

—— FOR DIPPING ——

Have ready some cooked chipolata sausages, cubes of cheese and crusty bread cubes, muffin cubes or potato fritters for the children. For vegetarians, omit bacon and serve fondue with veggie sausages or burgers.

—— COOK'S HINT ——

This fondue can be varied by using other varieties of baked beans, or by adding 75 g (3 oz) grated Edam cheese.

CREAMY CHEESE FONDUE WITH CRUDITÉS

SERVES 5–6

This is a lovely mild and creamy fondue – an ideal lunch for the children to enjoy out of doors on a sunny day.

25 g (1 oz) butter
25 g (1 oz) plain flour
450 ml (¾ pint) milk
125 g (4 oz) Philadelphia cream cheese, cubed

175 g (6 oz) Red Leicester cheese, grated
6 tablespoons double cream
½ teaspoon dry mustard
salt and white pepper

1 Melt the butter in the fondue pan on the hob and blend in the flour, stirring, for 1 minute.
2 Gradually add the milk, stirring between each addition, then bring to the boil, stirring constantly until the sauce has thickened.
3 Remove the fondue pan from the heat and mix in the cheeses and cream. Beat until the cheeses have melted and the fondue is smooth.
4 Stir in the mustard, and salt and pepper to taste.
5 Transfer the fondue pan to its lighted spirit stove to keep warm.

FOR DIPPING

Arrange individual serving plates of mixed crisp fruit and vegetable crudités – to include, carrots and celery sticks, cherry tomatoes, spring onions, button mushrooms, wedges of apple, pineapple cubes and cooked new baby potatoes.

SWEET AND SOUR FONDUE

SERVES 4–5

This is a firm favourite with the children and can be served with very tempting 'dippers'.

450 ml (¾ pint) chicken stock or water
1½ tablespoons cornflour
3 teaspoons light soy sauce
3 teaspoons white wine vinegar
2 tablespoons light soft brown sugar

3 tablespoons tomato ketchup
a pinch of salt and pepper
200 g (7 oz) can of pineapple chunks in natural juice

1 Heat the chicken stock or water in the fondue pan on the hob, until just simmering.

2 In a small bowl blend together the cornflour, soy sauce, vinegar, sugar and ketchup until smooth. Stir this into the stock or water and cook until thickened. Season with salt and pepper.

3 Drain the pineapple chunks and stir the juice into the mixture in the fondue pan.

4 Transfer the fondue pan to its lighted spirit stove to keep warm.

———————————— FOR DIPPING ————————————

Offer a selection of the following tasty treats: frankfurter sausages, pineapple chunks, cubes of ham, luncheon meat or cheese, pieces of cooked fish fingers or chicken nuggets. Allow a total of 175 g (6 oz) per child. Serve with prawn crackers.

RUM TUM TIDDY, RINK TUM DITTY

———————————— SERVES 5 ————————————

. . . or in other words, an early American version of a Welsh Rarebit! You can either serve this straight from the fondue pan, or spoon the mixture onto slices of toast and grill it. Either way, it is tasty.

25 g (1 oz) butter
1 tablespoon chopped onion
250 g (8 oz) tomatoes, peeled,
de-seeded and chopped
1 teaspoon caster sugar

a pinch of ground white pepper
150 ml (¼ pint) milk
375 g (12 oz) Cheddar cheese, grated
1 egg, beaten

1 Melt the butter in the fondue pan on the hob over a low heat and cook the onion for 5 minutes, or until golden.

2 Stir in the tomatoes, sugar and pepper. Add the milk and heat to just simmering.

3 Gradually add the cheese, stirring after each addition, to help the cheese melt.

4 Beat in the egg and cook, stirring, for a couple more minutes until the mixture is smooth and creamy.

5 Transfer the fondue pan to its lighted spirit stove to keep warm over a low flame.

———————————— FOR DIPPING ————————————

Serve this with cubes of french bread, crumpet cubes or toast fingers. A thin spread of yeast extract on the toast will add extra zest.

TOMATO FONDUE WITH CRISPY DIPS

—— SERVES 4–6 ——

Children will enjoy dipping their favourite cooked treats into this mild,
creamy fondue.

40 g(1½ oz) butter
40 g (1½ oz) plain flour
300 ml (½ pint) milk
*125 g (4 oz) mild Cheddar cheese,
grated*

125 ml (4 fl oz) tomato ketchup
*1 teaspoon Worcestershire sauce
(optional)*
a pinch of salt and pepper

1 Melt the butter in the fondue pan on the hob and add the flour. Cook,
 stirring, for one minute.
2 Gradually blend in the milk. Bring to the boil, stirring continuously until
 the sauce is thick and smooth.
3 Remove the pan from the heat and add the cheese and tomato ketchup and
 continue stirring until the cheese has melted. Season to taste with
 Worcestershire sauce, if using, salt and pepper.
4 Transfer the fondue pan to its lighted spirit stove to keep warm.

—— FOR DIPPING ——

Have a selection of cooked potato croquettes, chicken and fish nuggets,
toasted croûtons and pineapple chunks.
Pictured on page 51

MALLOW FUDGE FONDUE

—— SERVES 4 ——

175 g (6 oz) can evaporated milk
12 white marshmallows
½ teaspoon vanilla essence

125 g (4 oz) plain dessert chocolate
cocoa powder for dusting

1 Heat the evaporated milk in the chocolate fondue pan until just simmering.
 Cut the marshmallows into two and add half to the fondue, together with
 the vanilla essence.
2 Reduce the heat and stir constantly until the marshmallows have melted.
3 Break the chocolate into pieces, add them to the fondue pan and stir frequently until the mixture is smooth.
4 Add the remaining marshmallows and allow them to melt slightly on the
 surface of the fondue. Then gently swirl the mixture with a round-bladed
 knife to form an attractive pattern.

5 Carefully transfer the fondue pan onto its stand above the lighted candle. Sprinkle a little sifted cocoa powder onto the surface of the fondue. Keep warm.

──────────── FOR DIPPING ────────────

Offer sponge fingers, chocolate sponge or Sweet Choux Puffs (page 120).
Allow 50 g (2 oz) per person.
Chunks of banana, apple and pear also go well with this fondue. Allow 1–2 fruit per person.

BANANA FONDUE

──────────── SERVES 6 ────────────

3 ripe bananas
juice of 1 orange
1 teaspoon lemon juice
175 g (6 oz) can of sweetened
condensed milk

150 ml (¼ pint) whipping cream
1 small chocolate flake bar

1 Cut up the bananas and place in a blender or food processor with the orange and lemon juice, condensed milk and cream. Blend to a smooth purée.
2 Pour the purée into the fondue pan and heat gently until the fondue is warm.
3 Transfer the fondue pan to its lighted spirit stove to keep warm. Crumble the chocolate flake over the surface just before serving.

──────────── COOK'S HINT ────────────

For a more sophisticated adult fondue, replace the orange juice with 3 tablespoons rum.
Refrigerate any leftovers and enjoy as a chilled dessert.

──────────── FOR DIPPING ────────────

Offer a selection of chocolate sponge, chocolate cookies, fudge, Macaroons (page 123) and Schenkeli (page 116) for dipping, allowing 125 g (4 oz) per person.

*Left: Milk Chocolate Fondue with Eskimo Bananas (page 52); Right: Tomato Fondue
with Crispy Dips (page 48)*

MILK CHOCOLATE FONDUE
WITH ESKIMO BANANAS

——————— SERVES 4–5 ———————

This is a very indulgent fondue for children, so a little is enough! Refrigerate
any leftovers and use as a topping for ice cream.

125 g (4 oz) milk chocolate
25 g (1 oz) unsalted butter
1 tablespoon golden syrup

1 teaspoon grated lemon rind
4 tablespoons whipping cream

1 Break the chocolate into pieces and place in the chocolate fondue pan
together with the butter, syrup, lemon rind and cream.
2 Stir over a very low heat until smooth and glossy.
3 Transfer the fondue pan onto the stand above the lighted candle flame to
keep warm.

——————— FOR DIPPING ———————

Serve with Eskimo Bananas (page 124).
Segments of fresh orange and pear also go well; allow ½–1 fruit per person.

STRAWBERRY FONDUE

——————— SERVES 4–6 ———————

500 g (1 lb) fresh strawberries
2 tablespoons icing sugar
1 teaspoon grated orange peel

150 ml (¼ pint) whipping cream,
whipped lightly

1 Purée the strawberries and sugar together in a food processor or blender,
then sieve into the fondue pan. Stir in the orange peel and heat gently until
warmed through.
2 Swirl the cream into the strawberry purée.
3 Transfer the fondue pan to the lighted spirit stove, to keep warm over a
gentle heat.

——————— FOR DIPPING ———————

Allow 3–4 mini Cadbury's Chocolate Flakes per person. Sponge fingers,
marshmallows and tiny meringue shells also go well; allow 25–50 g (1–2 oz)
per person.

FONDUES for SPECIAL DIETS

PRAWN AND SCALLOP FONDUE PROVENÇALE

———— SERVES 4 ————

250 g (8 oz) scallops
250 g (8 oz) large prawns or scampi
fresh basil leaves
2 tablespoons olive oil
1 small onion, chopped finely
1 garlic clove, chopped finely
500 g (1 lb) tomatoes, peeled and
chopped

1 tablespoon tomato purée
2 teaspoons herbes de Provence
2 tablespoons white wine
900 ml (1½ pints) Court Bouillon
(page 113) or fish stock
salt and pepper

1 Separate the pink corals from the scallops, and slice the scallops into two. Divide the scallops and prawns or scampi between 4 plates and garnish with the basil leaves. Cover and chill until required.
2 Make the Provençale sauce: melt the butter in the fondue pan and cook the onion, garlic and tomatoes gently for 10 minutes.
3 Stir in the tomato purée, the herbs de Provence and white wine and season to taste with salt and pepper. Cover and simmer for 10 minutes.
4 Purée the sauce and pour into a serving bowl.
5 Rinse the fondue pan. Pour in enough court bouillon or stock to half or two-thirds fill the fondue pan and heat on the hob until just simmering. Transfer the fondue pan to its lighted spirit stove, adjust the flame to keep the bouillon or stock simmering.
6 Cook the scallops and prawns for 2 minutes, and the corals for 1 minute or until tender. Dip into the Sauce Provençal and serve with brown bread as a starter. Offer cucumber, avocado or pasta salad to make a main meal.

Prawn and Scallop Fondue Provençale (page 53)

FONDUE CHINOISE

An alternative method to cooking meats in hot oil is to use a well-flavoured stock or consommé. This means that people on low-fat diets can enjoy a meat fondue without consuming too many calories. This method is also known as Fondue Oriental.

FONDUE GITANE

Again as an alternative to oil, or indeed stock, this fondue uses sherry for cooking the meats or fish. The sherry can be a light cooking variety. Do not season it as it will reduce during boiling and then may taste too salty.

—— *RECIPES SUITABLE FOR COOKING BY THE CHINOISE OR GITANE METHOD* ——

Prawn and Scallop Fondue Provençale   Seafood Tempura
Chicken and Lemon Chinoise   Seafood Fondue
Tropical Gammon Fondue   Fondue Bourguignonne
Herby Lamb Fondue

———————— *SAUCES AND DIPS* ————————

You can adapt many of the sauces in this book by substituting low-calorie alternatives like yogurt and low-fat fromage frais for the high-calorie ingredients like mayonnaise and cream.

CHICKEN AND LEMON CHINOISE

———————— *SERVES 4* ————————

4 boneless chicken breasts, skinned
grated rind and juice of 2 lemons
1 tablespoon chopped sage
1 tablespoon chopped parsley
1 tablespoon light soy sauce

900 ml (1½ pints) chicken stock
a few fresh sage leaves
a few parsley stalks
6 black peppercorns, bruised slightly
black pepper

1 Cut the chicken breasts into bite-sized pieces. Place in a bowl.
2 Mix together the lemon rind and juice, herbs, soy sauce and pepper to taste. Pour this mixture over the chicken, cover and marinate in the refrigerator for 3–4 hours.

3 Drain the marinade into the fondue pan, add the stock, sage leaves, parsley stalks and peppercorns and bring to the boil. Transfer the fondue pan to its lighted spirit stove and allow to simmer gently.

4 Divide the chicken between 4 serving plates and cook the chicken in the simmering stock. Serve with a selection of sauces, and rice or noodles and salad.

────────── *FOR DIPPING* ──────────

Offer 2 or 3 of the following sauces: Cucumber and Yogurt Dip (page 107), Sweet Red Pepper Sauce (page 113), Spicy Tomato Dip (page 111), Oriental Sauce (page 112).

HARVEST VEGETABLE FONDUE

────────── *SERVES 4–6* ──────────

This is really a rich vegetable purée, using full-flavoured root vegetables. It is ideal for vegetarians and low in calories.

1 tablespoon vegetable oil
25 g (1 oz) butter
1 teaspoon mild curry powder (optional)
250 g (8 oz) carrots, chopped
250 g (8 oz) celeriac, chopped
250 g (8 oz) swede, chopped
1 small turnip, chopped
1 medium-size potato, chopped

1 medium-size onion, chopped
300 ml (½ pint) hot stock or Court Bouillon (page 113)
a pinch of ground nutmeg
2 tablespoons low-fat fromage frais
1 tablespoon chopped chives to garnish
salt and pepper

1 Heat the oil and butter together in a large pan. Stir in the curry powder (if using) and cook for 1 minute.

2 Add the vegetables, cover and cook for 4–5 minutes, shaking the pan occasionally.

3 Pour on the hot stock or bouillon, bring to the boil and then simmer for 25 minutes or until very tender. Leave to cool slightly, then sieve into the fondue pan.

4 Place the fondue pan over its lighted spirit stove and warm through. Season to taste with the nutmeg, and salt and pepper to taste. Stir in the fromage frais and garnish with the chives.

────────── *FOR DIPPING* ──────────

Offer cubes of bread, sesame seed biscuits or Gruyère Moons (page 116) and button mushrooms.

LOW-CALORIE CHEESE FONDUE

—— SERVES 4 ——

½ small onion
250 ml (8 fl oz) semi-skimmed milk
250 g (8 oz) half-fat Cheddar cheese,
grated
75 g (3 oz) low-fat cream cheese with
chives

3 tablespoons vodka or white wine
3 teaspoons cornflour
a pinch of dry mustard
ground black pepper

1 Rub the inside of the fondue pan with the cut onion. Pour in the milk and
   bring to the boil on the hob.
2 Reduce the heat and gradually add the cheeses, stirring until melted.
3 In a small bowl, blend the vodka or wine with the cornflour and stir this
   into the fondue. Continue to stir over a gentle heat until the mixture thickens. Season to taste with the mustard and pepper.
4 Transfer the fondue pan to its lighted spirit stove to keep warm.

—— FOR DIPPING ——

Offer a large selection of crisp vegetable crudités – cauliflower florets, carrot,
celery, cucumber and red pepper sticks, button mushrooms, radishes and
spring onions. Also serve apple and pear wedges and bread cubes.

SEAFOOD FONDUE WITH
APPLE AND HORSERADISH RELISH

—— SERVES 6 ——

750 g–1 kg (1½–2 lb) firm-fleshed
white fish and shellfish e.g. cod,
halibut, monkfish, hake, tuna,
scallops, prawns
a good fish stock or Court Bouillon
(page 113)
APPLE AND HORSERADISH RELISH
500 g (1 lb) Bramley apples, chopped

6 tablespoons water
1 strip of lemon peel
1 tablespoon clear honey
2 tablespoons horseradish relish
TO GARNISH
2 lemons, cut into wedges
fresh chervil

1 Cut the fish into thin slices or cubes. Divide the fish between 6 individual
   plates and garnish with the lemon wedges and chervil. Cover and
   refrigerate until required.

2 Place the apples in a saucepan with the water and lemon peel, cover and cook until the apples are reduced to a pulp.

3 Discard the lemon peel and stir in the honey and horseradish relish. Leave to cool.

4 Half to two-thirds fill the fondue pan with the stock or court bouillon; bring to the boil and then carefully transfer the fondue pan to its lighted spirit stove to simmer over a medium flame.

5 Individually spear the fish into the simmering stock or bouillon for a few minutes or until just cooked and then into the Apple and Horseradish Relish or one or two of those below.

-------------------- FOR DIPPING --------------------

Offer a choice from the following: Tartare Sauce (page 105), Quick Hollandaise Sauce (page 110), Cucumber and Yogurt Dip (page 107), Oriental Sauce (page 112), Sweet and Sour Barbecue Sauce (page 112), Green Goddess Dressing (page 106), Thousand Island Dip (page 106).

MUSHROOMS IN WHITE WINE

-------------------- SERVES 4–5 --------------------

50 g (2 oz) butter
2 tablespoons vegetable oil
2 large onions, sliced finely
500 g (1 lb) mushrooms, sliced thickly

450 ml (¾ pint) dry white wine
a bouquet garni
1 tablespoon chopped parsley
salt and pepper

1 Heat the butter and oil in the fondue pan on the hob and cook the onions over a gentle heat for 10 minutes or until softened, but not coloured.

2 Toss in the sliced mushrooms, increase the heat and cook for a further 2 minutes, stirring frequently.

3 Pour in the wine, add the bouquet garni and simmer until the wine has reduced by approximately one-third.

4 Remove and discard the bouquet garni, and season to taste with salt and pepper. Sprinkle on the chopped parsley.

5 Transfer the fondue pan to its lighted spirit stove to keep warm.

-------------------- FOR SERVING --------------------

Serve bowls of freshly grated cheese and crisp-cooked bacon pieces (allow 50 g (2 oz) per person), crispy garlic croûtons and french bread. While the croûtons and bread can be dipped in the sauce, the mushrooms should be ladled into warmed individual bowls and sprinkled with the cheese and bacon.

Mop up any remaining juices in the fondue pan with bread.

FRUITS OF THE FOREST FONDUE

SERVES 6–8

You can use a combination of fresh, frozen or, as in this recipe, canned red fruits and berries, but do adjust the sweetness level accordingly. The warm fruits may be ladled into bowls and served with vanilla ice cream.

375 g (12 oz) can raspberries in natural juice
375 g (12 oz) can red cherries, pitted and drained
375 g (12 oz) can blackberries, drained

2 tablespoons icing sugar, sifted
2 tablespoons brandy or kirsch
2 tablespoons cornflour
150 ml (¼ pint) low-fat fromage frais or natural yogurt

1 Sieve or purée the raspberries and make up to 300 ml (½ pint) with the natural juice. Place in the fondue pan with the cherries and blackberries.
2 Stir in the icing sugar and place the fondue pan on the hob over a moderate heat to warm through.
3 In a small bowl, blend together the brandy or kirsch and cornflour and stir into the fondue. Continue to cook for 2–3 minutes, stirring, until the mixture thickens slightly.
4 Transfer the fondue pan to its lighted spirit stove. Stir in the fromage frais or natural yogurt, and keep warm until required.

FOR DIPPING

Offer a selection of pink and white marshmallows, chunks of banana, tiny meringue shells and ratafia biscuits.
Pictured on the title page

CAROB FONDUE

SERVES 4–6

Carob is a pod of a tree prolific all over the Mediterranean area. It has a natural sweetness, no caffeine, is full of vitamins and minerals and is an excellent substitute for cocoa powder or chocolate. So if you want the taste of chocolate but without the caffeine, start experimenting with carob.

2 tablespoons cornflour
2 tablespoons carob powder
2 tablespoons soft brown sugar
425 g (14 oz) can pears or apricots

200 ml (7 fl oz) milk
25 g (1 oz) butter
a few drops of vanilla essence

1 Blend the cornflour, carob powder and sugar in the chocolate fondue pan with a little of the canned juice until smooth. Reserve the fruit and gradually blend in the remaining juice and the milk.
2 Place the fondue pan on the hob over a low heat and bring the sauce to the boil, stirring constantly, until it thickens. Remove from the heat and beat in the butter and vanilla essence.
3 Transfer the fondue pan to its lighted spirit stove to keep warm over a low heat. Cut the reserved fruit into pieces and use for dipping.

———————— FOR DIPPING ————————

In addition, offer fresh fruit – apples, bananas, grapes and pineapple. Allow 175–250 g (6–8 oz) per person. Lemon sponge cake, Sweet Choux Puffs (page 120) or Macaroons (page 123) will also go well with this.

———————— COOK'S HINT ————————

If you prefer to use a carob bar, follow a conventional chocolate fondue recipe, substituting the chocolate for the carob, but do take care not to overheat the carob bar.
Some coffee essence can be added to give a mocha flavour.

BLACKCURRANT FONDUE WITH CASSIS

———————— SERVES 5–6 ————————

2 × 300 g (10 oz) cans blackcurrants
in natural juice
2 tablespoons icing sugar (or the
equivalent using a low-calorie
sweetener), sifted

2 tablespoons crème de cassis or kirsch
2 tablespoons cornflour

1 Pour the blackcurrants and their juice into the fondue pan. Place the pan on the hob over a moderate heat and warm through. Stir in the icing sugar or sweetener. Taste and add a little more, if necessary.
2 In a small bowl, blend together the crème de cassis or kirsch with the cornflour and stir this into the blackcurrants. Increase the heat slightly and cook, stirring, until the mixture thickens.
3 Transfer the fondue pan to its lighted spirit stove to keep warm.

———————— FOR DIPPING ————————

Cut a small, ripe honeydew melon into bite-sized pieces. Also offer bananas, pears and apples – allowing 1 piece of fruit per person. And serve marshmallows, marzipan and tiny meringues – in moderation!

SPICED APRICOT FONDUE

*2 × 375 g (12 oz) cans apricot halves
in apple juice
4 cloves
1 teaspoon ground cinnamon
a large pinch of ground allspice*

*2 tablespoons cornflour
300 ml (½ pint) half-fat cream or
fromage frais
a pinch of cinnamon to garnish*

1 In the fondue pan, warm through the apricot halves in their juice together with the cloves, cinnamon and the allspice. Leave to cool, remove and discard the cloves.
2 Purée the apricots and juice in a blender or food processor with the cornflour, until smooth.
3 Pour into the fondue pan and bring to the boil on the hob, stirring constantly until the purée has thickened.
4 Transfer the fondue pan to its lighted spirit stove to keep warm. Stir in the cream or fromage frais and sprinkle a little cinnamon on the surface.

— FOR DIPPING —

Offer chunks of banana and pear with grapes and raspberries – allow 175 g (6 oz) per person. Macaroons or Petits Fours (page 123), marzipan, sponge fingers and Schenkeli (page 116) also go well.

Spiced Apricot Fondue, with Macaroons and Petits Fours (page 123)

FONDUES
from
FAR AWAY

BAGNA CAUDA

A *bagna cauda*, or 'hot bath', is an anchovy dip, served warm with a selection of crisp vegetables. It is a favourite in the Italian region of Piedmont, and would be served in small individual bowls or the traditional earthenware Bagna Cauda cooking pot. To follow tradition, when nearly all the anchovy dip has gone, crack an egg into the pot, scramble it over a low heat and mop up the mixture with some bread. As this makes quite a small quantity, it is ideal for making in the chocolate fondue pan.

125 g (4 oz) butter
2 garlic cloves, crushed
2 × 50 g (2 oz) cans anchovies

about 100 ml (3½ fl oz) olive oil
freshly ground black pepper

1 Melt the butter in the fondue pan on the hob. Cook the garlic for 2 minutes. Drain the anchovies and reserve the oil.
2 Add the drained anchovies and cook over a gentle heat, working them into a paste with a wooden spoon. Mix well.
3 Make the reserved oil up to 125 ml (4 fl oz) with the olive oil and gradually beat it in. Cook gently for a further 5 minutes.
4 Transfer the fondue pan to its lighted spirit stove to keep warm over a low heat. Mix the dip thoroughly from time to time to stop it separating.

———— FOR DIPPING ————

Offer a selection of crisp vegetable crudités – carrot, celery and green or red peppers, cut into strips, cauliflower florets, radishes and daikon (or mooli). Plus lightly cooked asparagus, fennel and globe artichokes. Bread sticks could complete the dippers.

CRISPY CHINESE PRAWNS

——————————— SERVES 4 AS A MAIN COURSE, 8 AS A STARTER ———————————

Prawns can prove somewhat tricky to skewer onto the fondue fork – it may be necessary to skewer three or four on at one time, before dipping in the batter. Alternatively, the larger peeled Dublin Bay prawns or scampi would work very well.

500 g (1 lb) peeled large prawns
2 tablespoons lemon juice
1 teaspoon light soy sauce
1 small egg, separated
250 ml (8 fl oz) water
125 g (4 oz) plain flour

1 teaspoon sesame oil
a pinch of salt
600 ml (1 pint) vegetable oil for frying
TO GARNISH:
2 lemons, cut into wedges
8 spring onions, trimmed and curled

1 Dry the prawns, place in a bowl and pour over the lemon juice and soy sauce. Marinate for 10–15 minutes. Divide the prawns between individual serving plates and garnish with the lemon wedges and spring onion curls

2 In a bowl, mix together the egg yolk, water, flour, sesame oil and a little salt with a balloon whisk until smooth. Cover and leave to stand until required.

3 Just before serving, whisk the egg white until it forms soft peaks and quickly fold this into the batter. Take the bowl of batter to the table.

4 Heat the oil in the fondue pan. Carefully transfer the pan to its lighted spirit stove to keep hot.

5 Each guest can now spear a prawn onto the fondue fork, dip it in the batter and then into the hot oil. The prawns will only need cooking for 1–2 minutes or until golden brown and crisp.

——————————— FOR DIPPING ———————————

Have ready an assortment of dips, including: Oriental Sauce (page 112), Sweet and Sour Barbecue Sauce (page 112), Tartare Sauce (page 105), Green Goddess Dressing (page 106).
Commercially prepared Chinese plum sauce, hoisin sauce and light soy or teriyaki sauce will also go well.

——————————— COOK'S HINT ———————————

If you want to cut down on the quantity of prawns, replace some of the prawns with button mushrooms, pieces of aubergine or courgette, or lightly cooked florets of cauliflower and broccoli.

SKEWERED CHINESE DUCK
WITH PLUM SAUCE

—————— *SERVES 4* ——————

4 boneless duck breasts, skinned
4 tablespoons light soy sauce
2 tablespoons brown sugar
1 teaspoon salt
1 teaspoon sesame seed oil
1 teaspoon sesame seeds
1 teaspoon Chinese 5-spice powder
1 garlic clove, chopped finely
1 cm (½-inch) piece of fresh root
ginger, chopped finely

8 spring onions, trimmed and curled,
to garnish
600 ml (1 pint) oil for frying
PLUM SAUCE
6 tablespoons Chinese plum sauce
1 tablespoon tomato purée
1 tablespoon light soy sauce
1 teaspoon chopped root ginger

1 Cut the duck breasts into 1 cm (½-inch) strips.
2 In a large bowl, mix the remaining ingredients together (except the oil for frying) and stir in the duck strips. Cover and marinate in the refrigerator for 4–6 hours.
3 To make the plum sauce: place the Chinese plum sauce, tomato purée, light soy sauce and root ginger in a small saucepan and heat gently, stirring occasionally, until the sauce is smooth. Keep warm.
4 Drain the duck pieces and divide between 4 plates. Garnish with spring onions.
5 Heat the oil in the fondue pan, and carefully transfer the pan to its lighted spirit stove to keep hot.
6 Skewer the duck onto the fondue forks and cook until crisp. Transfer to an eating fork to dip in the plum sauce.

————————— FOR DIPPING —————————

Other sauces are also delicious with the duck. Try a couple of the following:
Oriental Sauce (page 112), Spicy Tomato Dip (page 111), Cumberland Sauce
(page 111), Peanut Sauce (page 72), Sesame Sauce (page 77).

SHABU SHABU

This is the Japanese version of the Mohammedan Fire Kettle or Mongolian Hot Pot – a delicious yet plain and simple way of cooking meat and vegetables in a simmering broth. The name 'Shabu Shabu' apparently comes from the swishing sound made as slices of beef are swirled around in the steaming liquid.

500 g (1 lb) sirloin of beef
250 g (8 oz) fillet of lamb
50 g (8 oz) chicken breast, skinned
12 button mushrooms
12 spring onions, cut into 5 cm (2-inch) lengths
1 red pepper, de-seeded and cut into strips
250 g (8 oz) canned bamboo shoots

125 g (4 oz) mange tout
1 bunch of watercress
125 g (4 oz) fine egg noodles, broken up
6 Chinese leaves, shredded
1 carrot, sliced finely
2 teaspoons chopped fresh root ginger
900 ml (1½ pints) good chicken stock or consommé

1 Cut the beef, lamb and chicken into paper-thin slices. This is easier if the meat has been partially frozen. Divide between 6 dinner plates.

2 Divide the mushrooms, spring onions, red pepper, bamboo shoots, mange tout and watercress between 6 plates. Cover and chill until required.

3 Soak the egg noodles in boiling water for 3–4 minutes, then drain and transfer to a serving bowl.

4 Place the Chinese leaves, carrot and ginger in the fondue pan. Pour in enough stock or consommé to half to two-thirds fill it and heat on the hob until just boiling.

5 Transfer the fondue pan carefully to its lighted spirit stove over a high enough flame to maintain a steady simmer.

6 Either using the fondue fork, chopsticks or a Chinese wire strainer, individually cook pieces of meat and chicken and the vegetables in the stock. Then dip the food in a selection of sauces.

7 When all the cooking is completed, add the noodles to the fondue pan to heat through, then ladle the noodles, vegetables and stock into bowls and serve as a soup.

———— FOR DIPPING ————

Have ready small bowls of commercially prepared soy sauce, hoisin sauce, yellowbean sauce, chilli sauce and Tabasco sauce, a bowl of dry sherry and sesame oil. Guests can make their own blend of sauce on their plate to dip the food into.

ITALIAN FONDUTA WITH PASTA

SERVES 4

Originally made with Fontina cheese and white truffles, this Italian version would be served with polenta – a Roman speciality – or, as in this version, spooned over bowls of cooked pasta.

2 eggs, beaten
75 g (3 oz) butter, diced
250 g (8 oz) Gruyère cheese, grated
125 g (4 oz) dolcelatte cheese, cubed
50 g (2 oz) parmesan cheese, grated
6 tablespoons double cream

6 tablespoons dry white wine
a pinch of nutmeg
salt and pepper
250 g (8 oz) tagliatelle, cooked
fresh basil leaves to garnish

1 Pour the beaten eggs into the fondue pan. Mix in the butter, cheeses, cream and wine.
2 Cook on the hob, stirring constantly over a very low heat, until the cheeses begin to melt and the mixture starts to thicken. Do not allow to boil.
3 Meanwhile, cook the pasta according to pack instructions until just 'al dente' or still firm. A tablespoon of vegetable oil added to the cooking water will help prevent the pasta from sticking together.
4 Transfer the fondue pan to its stand to keep warm over a low flame. Stir occasionally.
5 Spoon the Fonduta over bowls of hot, cooked tagliatelle. Garnish with a sprig of fresh basil.

FOR DIPPING

Ciabatta bread.

CHILLI CHEESE DIP

———— *SERVES 6* ————

This is a Mexican dip, and it is also an excellent recipe for using up leftover 'Picadillo' (spiced minced beef sauce) or your own version of chilli con carne.

1 tablespoon vegetable oil
1 medium-size onion, chopped finely
1 garlic clove, chopped finely
250 g (8 oz) minced beef
1–2 teaspoons chilli powder
¼ teaspoon ground cinnamon
¼ teaspoon ground cumin
¼ teaspoon caster sugar

a pinch of ground cloves
1 jalapeno pepper or chilli, de-seeded and chopped finely
2 tablespoons tomato purée
425 g (14 oz) can chopped tomatoes
25 g (1 oz) raisins
½ teaspoon salt
500 g (1 lb) Cheddar cheese, grated

1 Heat the oil in the fondue pan and cook the onion and garlic until softened. Add the minced beef and continue cooking until the meat has browned.
2 Sprinkle in the chilli powder, cinnamon, cumin, sugar and cloves and cook for a further minute.
3 Add the jalapeno pepper or chilli, tomato purée, chopped tomatoes, raisins and salt. Mix together thoroughly.
4 Cook, covered, over a low heat for 1 hour, stirring occasionally. Leave to cool slightly.
5 Process in a food processor or mash until as smooth as possible. Return the mixture to the clean fondue pan and reheat.
6 Add the cheese gradually, allowing the cheese to melt completely before the next addition.
7 Transfer the fondue pan to its lighted spirit stove to keep warm.

———— FOR DIPPING ————

Serve with corn or tortilla chips, warm pieces of pitta bread, fresh tomato wedges and chunks of ripe avocado pear.

———— COOK'S HINT ————

Do take care to wash your hands thoroughly after handling fresh chillies.

SEAFOOD AND VEGETABLE TEMPURA

--------- *SERVES 4–6* ---------

'Tempura' is a name the Japanese have given to an adopted cooking technique – deep frying. The Chinese and Europeans probably introduced this technique to them and they have refined it to standards of elegant perfection.

4 plaice fillets, skinned
250 g (8 oz) fresh salmon or trout
fillets
2 medium-size squid, cleaned
250 g (8 oz) scampi tails
4 tablespoons seasoned flour
8 button mushrooms, halved
1 small aubergine, sliced
250 g (8 oz) broccoli florets
1 large red pepper, de-seeded and cut
into 8
125 g (4 oz) mange tout

BATTER
2 eggs, beaten
200 ml (7 fl oz) ice-cold water
125 g (4 oz) plain flour
50 g (2 oz) cornflour
600 ml (1 pint) safflower oil for frying
ACCOMPANIMENT
2 limes, quartered
5 cm (1-inch) piece of fresh root
ginger, grated
250 g (8 oz) daikon or mooli (Japanese
radish), peeled and grated
a little shoyu

1 Cut the plaice and salmon or trout into very thin strips. Cut the squid into rings. Dust all the fish lightly with the flour. Arrange either on a platter or divide between individual plates.
2 Arrange the vegetables on another platter or divide between the individual plates. Place a wedge of lime on each plate. Cover and chill the fish and vegetables until required.
3 To make the batter: mix together the eggs and water until light and foamy. Sift in the flour and cornflour and mix very briefly. Do not worry if there are one or two lumps. Place the batter on the dining table.
4 Heat the oil in the fondue pan. Carefully transfer the pan to its lighted spirit stove to keep hot.
5 Either using chopsticks or the fondue forks, dip the pieces of fish or vegetable in the batter and fry in the oil until the batter is crisp and golden. The fish should be tender too; but the vegetables are eaten crisp.
6 Dip the fish or vegetables into the accompanying dips and eat with a little of the ginger or daikon or mooli mixed together with a little shoyu.

--------- *FOR DIPPING* ---------

Serve with an equal mix of shoyu (Japanese soy sauce) and mirin (sweet rice wine) or one of the following: Oriental Sauce (page 112), Aioli Sauce (page 105), Quick Hollandaise Sauce (page 110), Spicy Tomato Dip (page 111), Red Pepper Sauce with Chilli (page 113).

Seafood and Vegetable Tempura, with Red Pepper Sauce with Chilli (page 113)

PORK AND LAMB SATAY WITH PEANUT SAUCE

SERVES 4–6

375 g (12 oz) pork fillet or
shoulder steaks
375 g (12 oz) boneless leg of lamb
600 ml (1 pint) oil for frying
MARINADE
2 tablespoons light soy sauce
2 garlic cloves, chopped finely
1 tablespoon oil
1 teaspoon chilli powder
½ teaspoon brown sugar
½ teaspoon cumin powder
½ teaspoon turmeric
½ teaspoon salt

PEANUT SAUCE
2 teaspoons vegetable oil
1 garlic clove, chopped finely
½ teaspoon ground ginger
½ teaspoon hot chilli powder
6 tablespoons crunchy peanut butter
300 ml (½ pint) boiling water
15 g (½ oz) creamed coconut
1 teaspoon soft light brown sugar
1 teaspoon lemon juice

1 Keeping the meats separate, cut the pork and lamb into bite-sized pieces
   and place in separate bowls.
2 Mix the marinade ingredients together and pour over the pork and lamb.
   Mix well, then cover and allow to stand at room temperature for 1 hour –
   or refrigerate for at least 3 hours.
3 To make the sauce: heat the oil in a small saucepan, add the garlic, ginger
   and chilli powder and peanut butter and cook for 1 minute. Remove from
   the heat and stir in the boiling water, creamed coconut, sugar and lemon
   juice. Bring to the boil, stirring, and simmer for 5–6 minutes. Serve warm.
4 Heat the oil in the fondue pan. Carefully transfer the pan to its lighted spirit
   stove to keep hot. Cook the pieces of lamb and pork in the hot oil and then
   transfer them to an eating fork to dip into the peanut sauce.

FOR DIPPING

Garlic Dip (page 107), Avocado Dip (page 108).

FONDUE INDIENNE WITH SAMBALS

SERVES 6

1 garlic clove, halved
25 g (1 oz) butter
1 small onion, chopped finely
2 teaspoons medium hot curry paste
250 ml (8 fl oz) dry white wine

2 teaspoons lemon juice
375 g (12 oz) Gruyère cheese, grated
1 tablespoon dry sherry
2 teaspoons cornflour
3 tablespoons natural yogurt

1 Rub the inside of the fondue pan with the cut garlic clove.
2 Melt the butter and add the onion. Cook for 4–5 minutes, until softened and golden brown. Stir in the curry paste and cook for a further minute.
3 Pour in the wine and lemon juice and heat gently until bubbling. Reduce the heat and gradually add the cheese. Stir frequently until the cheese has melted.
4 Blend the sherry and cornflour together, then stir into the cheese fondue and continue to cook for 2–3 minutes until the mixture thickens.
5 Transfer the fondue pan to its lighted spirit stove to keep warm. Just before serving, swirl in the yogurt.

FOR DIPPING

Prepare an assortment of 'sambals' – these are typical accompaniments to a spicy Indian meal.
For example: chunks of pineapple sprinkled with desiccated coconut; pieces of banana and apple, tossed in lemon juice; cubes of cooked potato, cooked celeriac or parsnip; poppadoms and naan bread.
Serve a bowl of mango chutney for dipping the bread or potato or fruits in, before dipping them into the fondue.

Fondue Indienne with Sambals, with Curried Bread Cubes (page 121)

CHINESE MONEY BAGS

SERVES 6–8

These small *dim sum* snacks are served in the teahouses of southern China. They are the perfect start to a meal, served with a Chinese plum or dipping sauce. The wuntun skins can be bought fresh or frozen from Chinese supermarkets.

Do not make these too far in advance because the bases will become soggy.

175 g (6 oz) minced chicken
75 g (3 oz) peeled prawns, chopped finely
2 smoked bacon rashers, chopped finely
1 tablespoon light soy sauce
1 tablespoon dry sherry
3 spring onions, chopped finely

1 teaspoon chopped fresh root ginger
1 teaspoon cornflour
1 teaspoon sesame oil
1 small egg, beaten
30 wuntun skins
600 ml (1 pint) oil for frying

1 Put all the ingredients (except the wuntun skins and the oil for frying) in a bowl and mix together well.
2 Place a teaspoon of the filling in the centre of each wuntun skin. Dampen the edges with water and either draw the skins up to form a gathered pouch or fold the skins in to form a sealed envelope. Place the bags on lightly floured plates.
3 Heat the oil in the fondue pan. Carefully transfer the fondue pan to its lighted spirit stove to keep hot.
4 Either use a Chinese wire strainer or carefully skewer the 'money' bags onto a fondue fork and fry for 2–3 minutes until crisp and golden.
5 Transfer to a serving plate to cool slightly before dipping ito a sauce, such as Sweet and Sour Barbecue (page 112), Spicy Tomato (page 111) or Oriental (page 112).

COOK'S HINT

When frying Chinese or Japanese foods, add a tablespoon of sesame oil to the oil used for frying, to enhance the flavour.

CHINESE CHICKEN WITH SESAME SAUCE

———————— SERVES 4 ————————

500 g (1 lb) boneless chicken breast,
skinned
1 teaspoon chilli powder
(or chilli sauce)
1 teaspoon caster sugar
1 tablespoon dry sherry (or rice wine)
2 teaspoons chopped fresh root ginger
2 spring onions, chopped finely
75 g (3 oz) plain flour
600 ml (1 pint) oil for frying

SESAME SAUCE
4 tablespoons light soy sauce
1 spring onion, chopped finely
1 garlic clove, chopped finely
1 teaspoon sesame seeds
1 teaspoon sesame oil
1 teaspoon caster sugar
1 teaspoon sherry vinegar
a pinch of hot chilli powder

1 Cut the chicken into 5 × 1 cm (2 × ½-inch) strips and put them in a large bowl.
2 Mix together the chilli powder, sugar, soy sauce, sherry or wine, ginger and spring onions. Pour onto the chicken and mix thoroughly. Cover and leave to stand for 1 hour.
3 Meanwhile, prepare the sauce: blend all the ingredients together and divide between 4 small bowls.
4 When ready to cook, drain the chicken and dust with enough of the flour to lightly coat the strips. Divide the chicken between 4 serving plates.
5 Heat the oil in the fondue pan. When the oil is the correct temperature, carefully transfer the pan to its lighted spirit stove. Skewer a piece of chicken onto the fondue fork and fry for 5–6 minutes, or until tender.
6 Transfer the chicken onto a table fork, and dip into the sauce before eating.

———————— FOR DIPPING ————————

As well as the sauce above, you may also like to serve the Oriental Sauce or Spicy Tomato Dip (pages 112 and 111).

SWORDFISH TERIYAKI

SERVES 6

Teriyaki is a way of marinating foods in a mixture of soy sauce, mirin (a sweet rice wine) and sake (a stronger rice wine), before cooking. This adapted recipe is a delicious way of cooking swordfish – or any firm-fleshed fish.

1 kg (2 lb) swordfish steaks, cut into
bite-sized pieces
125 ml (4 fl oz) light soy sauce
150 ml (¼ pint) dry sherry
6 tablespoons groundnut oil
2 garlic cloves, crushed

a pinch of ground black pepper
600 ml (1 pint) oil for frying
TO GARNISH:
6 spring onions, trimmed
1 lemon, cut into wedges

1 Place the cubes of fish in a shallow dish. Mix together the soy sauce, sherry, groundnut oil, garlic and pepper and pour this over the fish. Cover and chill for 6 hours.
2 Drain the fish and divide between 6 individual serving plates. Garnish with spring onions and wedges of lemon.
3 Heat the oil in the fondue pan. Carefully transfer the pan to its lighted spirit stove to keep hot.
4 Individually skewer the fish into the oil to cook for a few minutes. Transfer the fish to an eating fork and dip into the accompanying sauces.

FOR DIPPING

Garlic Dip (page 107), Sweet Red Pepper Sauce (page 113), Spicy Tomato Dip (page 111), Cucumber and Yogurt Dip (page 107), Oriental Sauce (page 112).

SWEET PEANUT DREAM

SERVES 4–5

This Chinese dessert tends to contradict the idea of serving fresh fruits – oranges, in particular – to cleanse the palate at the end of a Chinese meal. Let's compromise, and serve it with plenty of mouth-watering fruits.

50 g (2 oz) smooth peanut butter
900 ml (1½ pints) milk
4 tablespoons caster sugar

5 teaspoons rice flour or cornflour
4 tablespoons water

1 Place the peanut butter in the fondue pan on the hob. Gradually blend in the milk to make a smooth liquid.

2 Add the sugar and bring to the boil, whisking constantly until dissolved.
3 Blend the rice flour or cornflour with the water until smooth. Stir into the hot peanut mixture. Continue stirring until the mixture thickens.
4 Transfer the fondue pan to its lighted spirit stove to keep warm over a low heat.

──────────────── FOR DIPPING ────────────────

Serve this rich dessert with fresh juicy fruits – cubes of melon, pineapple, dessert apples and pears, lychees, mangoes and kiwifruit. Tiny Sweet Choux Puffs (page 120), marzipan and cubes of sponge cake also go well.

KESARI BUTH

──────────────── SERVES 4–5 ────────────────

This is a semolina and milk dessert from Sri Lanka. It may be eaten on its own, followed by a course of fresh local fruits – pineapple, mango and paw-paw.

50 g (2 oz) unsalted butter or ghee
125 g (4 oz) cashew nuts, chopped
    coarsely
seeds of 3 cardamom pods, crushed
75 g (3 oz) sultanas
5 tablespoons semolina

600 ml (1 pint) milk
75 g (3 oz) caster sugar
1 tablespoon rose-water
(or orange-blossom water)
6 tablespoons single cream

1 Heat the butter or ghee in the fondue pan and fry the cashew nuts until golden in colour. Drain and transfer to a plate.
2 Fry the cardamom seeds and sultanas for a minute, then drain and transfer to the plate.
3 Sprinkle the semolina into the pan and stir over a moderate heat until golden brown.
4 Gradually blend in the milk, add the sugar and continue to cook, stirring constantly until the mixture is smooth and creamy.
5 Return the cashew nuts, cardamom seeds and sultanas to the pan and stir in together with the flower-water and cream.
6 Transfer the fondue pan to its lighted spirit stove to keep warm over a low heat.

──────────────── FOR DIPPING ────────────────

Arrange an attractive platter of tropical fruits – pieces of banana, pineapple, mango, papaya, lychees and orange segments. Also offer pieces of plain, lemon or coconut-flavoured sponge cake.

FONDUES
for
SOPHISTICATION

TURKEY WITH LEMON SAUCE

SERVES 6

*750 g (1½ lb) boneless turkey
breast or fillets, skinned
1 tablespoon cornflour
grated rind of ½ lemon
ground black pepper
600 ml (1 pint) oil for frying
6 spring onions to garnish*

*LEMON SAUCE
2 teaspoons cornflour
grated rind and juice of ½ lemon
2 tablespoons clear honey
1 teaspoon stem ginger, chopped finely
2 teaspoons stem ginger syrup
½ teaspoon sesame oil
2 teaspoons light soy sauce
300 ml (½ pint) chicken stock*

1 Cut the turkey meat into 2.5 cm (1-inch) strips. Place in a bowl and sprinkle with the cornflour, lemon rind and plenty of ground black pepper. Arrange on 6 individual serving plates and garnish each with a spring onion. Cover and chill until required.

2 To make the lemon sauce: blend the cornflour with the lemon rind and juice, honey, stem ginger, syrup, sesame oil and soy sauce.

3 In a small saucepan, bring the chicken stock to a steady boil. Mix in the blended cornflour mixture and stir until the sauce has thickened. Transfer to individual serving bowls and keep warm.

4 Heat the oil in the fondue pan until at the correct temperature. Carefully transfer the pan to its lighted spirit stove to keep hot.

5 Skewer turkey pieces onto the fondue fork and cook in the hot oil for 3 minutes or until tender. Transfer the turkey to an eating fork and dip into the lemon sauce. Serve with plain boiled rice.

FOR DIPPING

Avocado Dip (page 108).

HERBY LAMB FONDUE

SERVES 4–6

Choose a boned leg of lamb for this recipe. It needs to be prepared a day in advance so that it has plenty of time to soak up the flavours of the marinade.

750 g–2 kg (1½–2 lb) lean lamb
2 garlic cloves, crushed
150 ml (¼ pint) red table wine
4 tablespoons red wine vinegar
4 tablespoons olive oil
6 juniper berries, crushed lightly
6 black peppercorns, crushed lightly

1 teaspoon mixed dried herbs
2 teaspoons dried rosemary
1 bay leaf, crumbled
½ teaspoon salt
600 ml (1 pint) oil for frying
fresh parsley or rosemary sprigs to garnish

1 Trim the meat of any fat and cut it into 2.5 cm (1-inch) cubes. Place in a large shallow dish.
2 In a screw-top jar, shake together the remaining ingredients (except the oil for frying) to make the marinade. Pour this over the lamb, coating all the pieces well.
3 Cover and marinate for 24 hours in the refrigerator. Turn the meat in the mixture occasionally.
4 Drain the meat and pat the cubes dry on pieces of paper towel. Arrange the meat on 4–6 individual serving plates, and garnish each with a sprig of fresh parsley or rosemary.
5 Heat the oil in the fondue pan. Carefully transfer the fondue pan to its lighted spirit stove.
6 Individually cook the lamb to your preferred degree and then transfer to an eating fork to enjoy with the dips. Accompany with a green salad and new potatoes or garlic bread.

FOR DIPPING

Offer a choice of at least 3 dips or sauces from the following: mint sauce, Aioli Sauce (page 105), Quick Hollandaise Sauce (page 110), Cumberland Sauce (page 111), Pesto Sauce (page 109), Mild Curry Sauce (page 109), Garlic Dip (page 107).

Herby Lamb Fondue (page 81), with Garlic Dip (page 107) and Cumberland Sauce (page 111)

CHICKEN AND FISH GOUJONS

SERVES 4 AS A MAIN COURSE, 8 AS A STARTER

Goujons – traditionally strips of breaded fish – can be prepared in advance. A combination of fish and chicken go well together and with similar dips. Plaice or sole make particularly delicious fish goujons.

375 g (12 oz) white fish fillets, skinned
375 g (12 oz) boneless chicken breasts, skinned
4 tablespoons seasoned flour
3 large eggs, beaten

175 g (6 oz) fresh white breadcrumbs
600 ml (1 pint) oil for frying
TO GARNISH
1 lemon, cut into wedges
sprigs of fresh parsley or tarragon

1 Wipe the fish fillets and cut them diagonally across into long strips, approximately 1 cm (½ inch) wide. Toss the strips in the seasoned flour. Dip the strips in the beaten egg and then in the breadcrumbs. Repeat the cutting and coating with the chicken breasts. Refrigerate until required.
2 When ready to cook, divide the goujons between 4 or 8 serving dishes and garnish with a wedge of lemon and parsley or tarragon.
3 Heat the oil in the fondue pan. Carefully transfer the pan to its lighted spirit stove to keep hot.
4 Individually cook the goujons until golden and crisp.

FOR DIPPING

Offer a choice of at least 3 dips or sauces from the following: Tartare Sauce (page 105), Tomato Mayonnaise (page 106), Quick Béarnaise Sauce (page 110), Green Goddess Dressing (page 106), Mild Curry Sauce (page 109), Aioli Sauce (page 105), Sweet Red Pepper Sauce (page 113), Blue Cheese Dip (page 108), Avocado Dip (page 108), Pesto Sauce (page 109), Sweet and Sour Barbecue Sauce (page 112).

COQUILLES SAINT-JACQUES FONDUE

SERVES 3–4 AS A MAIN MEAL, 6 AS A STARTER

Coquille is the French name for 'shell' but is also the name given to the scallop – one of the most nutritious and delicious of all shellfish. A small and slightly less expensive relative is the 'queenie' which is recommended for this recipe. Do not overcook the 'queenies' – they need only minutes!

25 g (1 oz) butter
50 g (2 oz) tiny button mushrooms
4 tablespoons Pernod or dry sherry
500 g (1 lb) scallops or 'queenies'
3 egg yolks

150 ml (¼ pint) double cream
1 tablespoon chopped fresh chives
a pinch of salt
a pinch of Cayenne pepper

1 Melt the butter in the fondue pan and cook the mushrooms for a few minutes. Pour in the Pernod or sherry and cook for a further minute or until the mushrooms have softened.

2 Meanwhile prepare the scallops or 'queenies'. Remove the coral (pink/orange) parts from the scallops and reserve. Cut the white part into thick slices (the queenies do not need cutting).

3 Blend the egg yolks with the cream and chives, and stir into the fondue pan together with the prepared scallops or 'queenies'. Cook, stirring constantly, for 2 minutes. The sauce will thicken slightly. Do not boil or the sauce will separate and be spoiled. Season with salt and Cayenne.

4 Transfer the fondue pan to its lighted spirit stove to keep warm over a low flame. Gently stir the mixture frequently.

5 Serve immediately – each guest can spear the mushrooms and scallops onto an individual plate.

FOR DIPPING

Simply offer cubes of white or brown bread to enjoy with the sauce.

CRAB FONDUE

—————— SERVES 4–5 ——————

Although white crab meat will give a better appearance, you can use a mix of
the white and dark meat and enjoy a stronger flavour.

50 g (2 oz) butter	1 tablespoon cornflour
4 spring onions, chopped finely	3 tablespoons dry sherry
300 ml (½ pint) milk	250 g (8 oz) crab meat, flaked
250 g (8 oz) samsoe cheese, grated	a pinch of ground mace
125 g (4 oz) cream cheese with chives, cubed	a pinch of ground nutmeg
	salt and pepper

1 Melt the butter in the fondue pan on the hob, and cook the spring onions
   for a minute, to soften slightly.
2 Pour in the milk and bring it to the boil.
3 Reduce the heat, and gradually add the cheeses, stirring constantly until
   melted.
4 In a small bowl, blend the cornflour with the dry sherry and stir this into
   the cheese mixture.
5 Stir in the crab meat, mace and nutmeg, and season to taste with salt and
   pepper.
6 Transfer the fondue pan to its lighted spirit stove to keep warm.

—————— FOR DIPPING ——————

Serve with cubes of Granary bread, crispy cooked baby sweetcorn, potato
cubes and cauliflower florets – allowing 250 g (8 oz) per person.

SEAFOOD FONDUE

—————— SERVES 4–5 ——————

This is really a version of *Fritto Misto di Mare* – an indulgence generally
enjoyed on Mediterranean holidays, but now, with the choice of more exotic
fish available, you don't need to travel too far to enjoy it!

750 g (1½ lb) mixed seafood, including haddock, whiting, squid (ask your fishmonger to prepare it), scampi, monkfish	600 ml (1 pint) oil for frying
	TO GARNISH
	2 lemons cut into wedges
75 g (3 oz) seasoned flour	fresh parsley sprigs

1 If you have chosen squid, it can be a little tough, so cook the rings in a pan of boiling water for 20 minutes, then drain and dry thoroughly. Wash and dry the remaining fish.

2 Place the flour in a large polythene bag and add the fish. Shake until all the fish is coated in the flour.

3 Divide the fish between 4–5 serving plates and garnish with lemon wedges and sprigs of parsley.

4 Heat the oil in the fondue on the hob, then transfer it to its lighted spirit stove to keep hot.

5 Skewer a piece of fish onto the fondue fork and cook the fish in the oil until crisp and golden brown.

6 Transfer the fish to a table fork and dip into a selection of sauces.

——————— *FOR DIPPING* ———————

Choose 2 or 3 sauces from the following: Tartare Sauce (page 105), Quick Béarnaise Sauce (page 110), Sour Cream and Chive Dip (page 107), Oriental Sauce (page 112), Garlic Dip (page 107).

NORMANDY FONDUE WITH CALVADOS

——————— *SERVES 4* ———————

1 garlic clove, halved
200 ml (7 fl oz) dry white wine
250 g (8 oz) Camembert cheese
125 g (4 oz) Port Salut or St Paulin
cheese, grated

1 tablespoon cornflour
3 tablespoons Calvados
a pinch of grated nutmeg
a pinch of ground white pepper
4 tablespoons single cream

1 Rub the cut side of the garlic clove around the inside of the fondue pan. Pour in the wine and heat until bubbling.

2 Meanwhile, cut away and discard the rind on the Camembert. Cut the cheese into thin slices and gradually add to the hot wine together with the Port Salut or St Paulin cheese, stirring constantly until melted.

3 Blend the cornflour with the Calvados and stir this into the fondue. Cook for 2 minutes, until the fondue is smooth and creamy. Season to taste with the nutmeg and pepper.

4 Transfer the fondue pan to its lighted spirit stove to keep warm. Swirl in the single cream just before serving.

——————— *FOR DIPPING* ———————

Offer cubes of french bread, apples and pears with this fondue.

ROQUEFORT FONDUE WITH FRESH PEARS

SERVES 4–6

This makes an excellent first course – although it may be tempting to eat too much and spoil the following course! Roquefort is a French blue-veined cheese; if you prefer, try the Italian Gorgonzola or a fine English Stilton. The combination of sweet dessert pears and piquant cheese works well.

1 garlic clove, halved
150 ml (¼ pint) dry white wine
250 g (8 oz) Port Salut or mild Cheddar cheese, grated
250 g (8 oz) Roquefort cheese, diced
2 teaspoons cornflour

4 tablespoons single cream
a pinch of ground nutmeg
a pinch of black pepper
6 ripe dessert pears, cut into bite-size pieces and covered until required

1 Rub the inside of the fondue pan with the cut side of the garlic. Pour in the wine and heat on the hob until just bubbling. Reduce the heat.
2 Gradually stir in the cheeses, until melted and blended.
3 Blend the cornflour with the cream. Stir into the cheese with the nutmeg and pepper and continue to heat gently, stirring constantly, until the mixture thickens. Check the seasoning.
4 Transfer the fondue pan to its lighted spirit stove to keep warm. Dip the pear pieces into the fondue.

FOR DIPPING

Also offer some cubed Granary bread or Parsley Biscuits (page 115).
Pictured on page 90

FLEMISH CHEESE FONDUE CAKES

MAKES 50–60

These delicious savouries are traditionally made in a fondue pan and need to be started 24 hours in advance. They are a little time consuming, but the outcome is delicious and worth the effort!

750 g (1½ lb) ripe Camembert cheese
125 g (4 oz) cornflour
200 ml (7 fl oz) milk
75 g (3 oz) unsalted butter
½ teaspoon salt
a pinch of ground white pepper

a pinch ground nutmeg
plain flour for dusting
2 eggs, beaten
125 g (4 oz) dry breadcrumbs
600 ml (1 pint) oil for frying

1 Cut away the rind from the cheese and cut the cheese into small pieces. Lightly grease and line a swiss roll tin 30 × 18 × 2.5 cm (12 × 7 × 1 inches) with greaseproof paper.

2 Blend the cornflour with half the milk to make a smooth paste. Gradually mix in the remaining milk. Pour into the fondue pan and stir over a gentle heat.

3 Add the cheese, the butter, salt, pepper and nutmeg and continue to heat gently, stirring constantly, until the cheese melts and the mixture becomes thick and creamy. (It will now come away from the sides of the fondue pan.)

4 Spread the mixture over the lined baking tray, so that it is approximately 2.5 cm (1-inch) thick. Leave to cool, then refrigerate for 6–12 hours to become firm.

5 Cut the cheese paste into small squares or triangles. Carefully remove them from the tin and dust them lightly with the flour.

6 Dip each square into the beaten egg, drain, then coat with the dry breadcrumbs to cover the cheese completely. Repeat with a second coating of egg and breadcrumbs. Chill until required.

7 Heat the oil in the fondue pan. Carefully transfer the pan to its spirit stove. Fry the fondue cakes in deep fat in the fondue pan (at the table, if you like), a few at a time, for 1–2 minutes or until crisp and golden. They should still be runny inside. Transfer to a serving plate, allowing 4–5 cakes as a starter or 8–10 as a main course.

———————— COOK'S HINT ————————

As this recipe makes a large quantity, once the cakes are coated in egg and breadcrumbs, open freeze half the quantity for up to 2 months. Thaw thoroughly before frying.

———————— FOR DIPPING ————————

Cumberland Sauce (page 111), Pesto Sauce (page 109), Spicy Tomato Dip (page 111).

Roquefort Fondue with Pears (page 88), with Parsley Biscuits (page 115)

PRALINE FONDUE

SERVES 5–6

75 g (3 oz) blanched almonds
75 g (3 oz) caster sugar
300 ml (½ pint) double cream

1 teaspoon cornflour
1 tablespoon water or a favourite
liqueur

1 To make the praline: place the almonds and sugar in a heavy-based frying pan and heat gently until the sugar dissolves. Increase the heat a little and cook, stirring, until the nuts are golden brown.
2 Pour the mixture onto an oiled baking tray and leave to cool and harden. Either crush the nut brittle with a rolling pin or grind coarsely in an electric coffee grinder. Store it in an airtight jar until required.
3 Heat the cream in the chocolate fondue pan until just scalding. Blend the cornflour with the water or liqueur and stir into the cream. Continue stirring until the mixture thickens slightly.
4 Stir in the praline. Transfer the chocolate fondue pan onto its stand above the lighted candle to keep warm.

FOR DIPPING

Chunks of fresh pineapple, banana and pear, fresh strawberries and peaches will go well with this. Allow 175 g (6 oz) per person. Cubes of chocolate sponge, tiny Sweet Choux Puffs (page 120) and baby meringues will also be delicious.

COFFEE COGNAC FONDUE

SERVES 6

A bar of chocolate with fruit and nuts can be used instead of plain chocolate to make this luxurious fondue.

1 tablespoon instant coffee granules
1 tablespoon caster sugar
250 g (8 oz) plain chocolate

150 ml (¼ pint) double cream
2 tablespoons cognac or coffee liqueur

1 In a small bowl mix together the coffee and sugar with a tablespoon of boiling water to form a smooth paste.
2 Break the chocolate into pieces and heat gently in the chocolate fondue pan together with the cream and coffee mixture. Stir frequently until smooth and creamy.
3 Add the cognac or liqueur. Transfer the fondue pan onto its stand above the lighted candle flame to keep warm.

FOR DIPPING

Offer an assortment of miniature brandy snaps, pieces of sponge cake, Macaroons (page 123) and tiny cubes of marzipan – allow a total of 50 g (2 oz) per person.

Also serve refreshing fresh fruit: pears, apricots, bananas, raspberries and strawberries, allowing 175 g (6 oz) per person. Prunes may be served, too.

BITTER CHOCOLATE AND ORANGE FONDUE

SERVES 5–6

250 g (8 oz) Bournville chocolate
rind of ½ orange, grated finely
150 ml (¼ pint) double cream

15 g (½ oz) unsalted butter
2 tablespoons Cointreau (optional)

1 Break the chocolate into pieces and heat very gently in the chocolate fondue pan together with the orange rind, double cream and butter. Stir occasionally.
2 Beat in the Cointreau. Transfer the fondue pan onto its stand above the lighted candle flame to keep warm.

FOR DIPPING

Offer a selection of fresh, chilled fruits – strawberries, apricots, peaches, bananas and kiwifruit will all taste delicious. Allow 175 g (6 oz) fruit per person.

As a contrast, offer Macaroons (page 123), flapjack, Sweet Choux Puffs (page 120) or Schenkeli (page 116).

FONDUES
as a
FINALE

CHOC 'O' NUT FONDUE

SERVES 4

250 g (8 oz) milk chocolate
150 ml (¼ pint) double cream

75 g (3 oz) toasted hazelnuts, chopped
coarsely

1 Break the chocolate into pieces and place in the chocolate fondue pan with the cream. Heat gently, stirring frequently, until smooth and creamy.
2 Stir in the toasted hazelnuts.
3 Transfer the chocolate fondue pan onto its stand above the lighted candle flame to keep warm.

FOR DIPPING

Offer pieces of fresh fruit – apples, pineapple, pears, banana and orange segments – allow 1 whole fruit per person.
Also offer tiny meringue shells, pieces of brioche or croissant and plain danish pastries.

Choc 'o' Nut Fondue

JAMAICAN CALYPSO FONDUE

———— SERVES 6 ————

When fresh pineapple is plentiful and not too expensive, the flesh can be scooped out, puréed and used in place of canned. The pineapple shells make superb 'baskets' for serving the dipping ingredients in.

2 × 400 g (14 oz) cans crushed pineapple	2 tablespoons cornflour
4 tablespoons caster sugar	2 tablespoons lemon juice
300 ml (½ pint) whipping cream	4 tablespoons Malibu or white rum (optional)

1 Place the pineapple and its juice, the sugar and cream in the fondue pan. Heat gently, stirring occasionally.
2 Blend the cornflour with the lemon juice and Malibu or rum (if using). Add to the fondue, stirring constantly until the mixture thickens slightly.
3 Transfer the fondue to the lighted spirit stove to keep warm.

———— FOR DIPPING ————

Offer ginger and chocolate biscuits and sponge and Macaroons (page 123). Allow 50 g (2 oz) per person. Bite-size pieces of fresh coconut are also quite delicious!

HONEY ALMOND FONDUE

———— SERVES 4–5 ————

250 g (8 oz) white chocolate	75 g (3 oz) toasted almonds, chopped finely
150 ml (¼ pint) double cream	1 tablespoon amaretto liqueur (optional)
4 tablespoons clear honey	

1 Break the chocolate into pieces and place in the chocolate fondue pan with the cream and honey. Heat gently, stirring frequently, until smooth and creamy.
2 Stir in the chopped nuts and the amaretto (if using).
3 Transfer the chocolate fondue pan onto its stand above the lighted candle to keep warm.

———— FOR DIPPING ————

Offer an assortment of fresh fruit and dried apricots, plus pieces of plain sponge, sponge fingers, Petits Fours (page 123) or Schenkeli (page 116).

ORCHARD FRUIT FONDUE
WITH CINNAMON CREAM

———————— SERVES 4–6 ————————

Fresh apples and pears are poached, at the table, in a delicious cream. A perfect ending to a meal.

125 g (4 oz) granulated sugar
5 cm (2-inch) strip of orange peel
5 cm (2-inch) strip of lemon peel
½ stick cinnamon
2 cloves
1 cardamom pod
450 ml (¾ pint) water
4 Cox's dessert apples
4 firm dessert pears
3 tablespoons lemon juice

2 tablespoons brandy or Calvados
(optional)
CINNAMON CREAM
150 ml (¼ pint) double cream
rind of 1 small orange, grated finely
3 tablespoons sweet sherry, cider or
apple juice
1–2 tablespoons caster sugar
½ teaspoon ground cinnamon

1 First make the cinnamon cream: in a bowl, whisk together all the ingredients until light and thick. Transfer to a serving bowl and chill until required.
2 Place the granulated sugar, orange and lemon peel, cinnamon, cloves and the cardamom pod in the fondue pan. Pour in the water. Heat gently, stirring occasionally, until the sugar has dissolved.
3 Meanwhile, cut the fruit into segments and toss in the lemon juice. Divide between 4–6 serving plates.
4 Bring the syrup to a steady boil for 2 minutes. Carefully transfer the fondue pan to the lighted spirit stove.
5 Stir in the brandy or Calvados, if using. Adjust the lighted stove to keep the syrup at a steady simmer.
6 Poach the fruit in the syrup for 3–4 minutes or until just tender. Transfer the fruit segments onto a dessert fork and dip into the cinnamon cream.

———————— COOK'S HINT ————————

Other firm fruits can be poached instead of the apples and pears. Try fresh pineapple or banana chunks, cherries and figs, when in season, for a change. A tangy Orange Sauce (page 114) will complement the fruit and cinnamon cream as an alternative 'dipper'.

Orchard Fruit Fondue with Cinnamon Cream (page 97)

MISSISSIPPI CHOCOLATE FONDUE

——————— *SERVES 4* ———————

¼ teaspoon ground cinnamon
1 tablespoon soft brown sugar
50 g (2 oz) raisins

2 tablespoons dark rum
250 g (8 oz) plain chocolate
150 ml (¼ pint) double cream

1 In a small bowl, mix together the cinnamon, brown sugar, raisins and rum. Leave to stand for 30 minutes.
2 Break the chocolate into pieces and place in the chocolate fondue pan with the cream. Place over a very low heat and stir frequently until the chocolate melts.
3 Add the sugar and raisin mixture and stir thoroughly until smooth and blended.
4 Transfer the fondue pan onto its stand above the lighted candle flame, to keep warm.

——————— *FOR DIPPING* ———————

Offer chunks of fresh pineapple, bananas or raspberries. Allow 175 g (6 oz) per person.
Macaroons (page 123) or Peanut Cookies (page 117) will also be a delicious accompaniment, or small squares of flapjack.

BUTTERSCOTCH FONDUE

SERVES 5–6

50 g (2 oz) unsalted butter
175 g (6 oz) demerara sugar
2 tablespoons golden syrup
½ teaspoon grated lemon rind

1 teaspoon lemon juice
2 tablespoons cornflour
425 g (14 oz) can evaporated milk

1 Gently heat together the butter, sugar, syrup, lemon rind and juice in the fondue pan on the hob until the sugar has dissolved. Allow the mixture to boil for 1 minute.
2 Blend the cornflour to a smooth paste with some of the evaporated milk. Stir the remainder into the sugar mixture. Cook for 2–3 minutes until just simmering.
3 Stir in the blended cornflour, then bring the butterscotch fondue to the boil, stirring constantly until smooth and thick.
4 Transfer the fondue pan to its lighted spirit stove to keep warm.

FOR DIPPING

Offer a selection of fresh chilled fruit – bananas, apples and pears, cut into bite-size chunks. Allow 1–2 fruit per person. Plain and chocolate cookies also go well with this fondue; allow 3–4 biscuits per person.

CARAMEL FONDUE

SERVES 5–6

200 g (7 oz) granulated sugar
2 tablespoons tepid water

200 ml (7 fl oz) double cream
1 tablespoon cornflour

1　Heat the granulated sugar in the fondue pan on the hob. When it begins to dissolve, bubble and darken, stir continuously until it is a dark liquid syrup.
2　Remove the fondue pan from the heat and add the tepid water. The syrup may splutter at this stage. Continue stirring until smooth.
3　Return the pan to a moderate heat and stir in the double cream.
4　Blend the cornflour with a little water, and add this to the caramel cream. Now stir constantly until the mixture thickens.
5　Transfer the fondue pan to its lighted spirit stove to keep warm.

FOR DIPPING

Offer segments of fresh orange and wedges of pear; allow 1 fruit per person.

ST CLEMENT'S FONDUE

SERVES 5–6

175 g (6 oz) can evaporated milk,
chilled
125 g (4 oz) caster sugar
2 tablespoons cornflour

juice of 2 oranges
rind of 1 orange, grated finely
grated rind and juice of ½ lemon
50 g (2 oz) unsalted butter

1　In a bowl, whisk together the evaporated milk, sugar, cornflour, orange and lemon juice and rind, until light and foamy. (An electric whisk or rotary beater is best.)
2　Pour the creamy mixture into the fondue pan and stir constantly over a moderate heat, until the mixture thickens slightly.
3　Cut the butter into small pieces and add to the fondue pan. Stir until the butter has melted into the creamy mixture.
4　Transfer the fondue pan to the lighted spirit stove to keep warm over a gentle heat.

FOR DIPPING

Offer a selection of fresh fruits – pineapple chunks, banana, kiwifruit and strawberry. Allow 175 g (6 oz) per person. Chocolate or ginger cookies, fudge, or sponge cake also go well. Allow 50–75 g (2–3 oz) per person.

LEMON FOAM FONDUE

SERVES 8–10

As this recipe makes a good quantity, it's ideal to serve at a buffet, with a bowl of fresh strawberries. Any leftovers can be stored in a screw-top jar in the refrigerator and could be served as a delicious topping to ice cream.

2 × 175-g (6 oz) cans of evaporated milk, chilled
75 g (3 oz) unsalted butter
175 g (6 oz) caster sugar

2 teaspoons grated lemon rind
4 tablespoons lemon juice
3 teaspoons cornflour

1 In a bowl, whisk the chilled evaporated milk until it is thick and creamy. Leave in the refrigerator until required.
2 Melt the butter in the fondue pan. Add the sugar, lemon rind and juice and stir until the sugar has dissolved.
3 Blend the cornflour with a tablespoon of cold water and mix into the lemon sauce, stirring constantly until it thickens slightly.
4 Gradually whisk in the chilled evaporated milk (use a balloon whisk to help make it foamy).
5 Transfer the fondue pan to its lighted spirit stove to keep warm.

FOR DIPPING

Serve whole strawberries or raspberries with this fondue, allowing 75–125 g (3–4 oz) per person. Marshmallows, Peanut Cookies (page 117), brandy snaps, Schenkeli (page 116) and chocolate sponge will also go well with the lemon flavour.
Pictured on page 118

FONDUE
SAUCES
and
DIPS

BASIC MAYONNAISE

——————— MAKES 300 ML (½ PINT) ———————

2 egg yolks
1 teaspoon salt
1 teaspoon prepared Dijon mustard
a pinch of ground white pepper

2 tablespoons white wine vinegar or
lemon juice
300 ml (½ pint) groundnut oil

1 Place the egg yolks, salt, mustard, pepper and 1 tablespoon of vinegar or lemon juice in a small bowl. Using an electric or balloon whisk, mix together until creamy.
2 Drop by drop, start to whisk in the oil. Once the mayonnaise begins to thicken, add the oil in a thin steady stream, whisking constantly.
3 Once all the oil is added, add the remaining vinegar or lemon juice to thin the mixture down a little. Season to taste.
4 Refrigerate the mayonnaise in a screw-top jar for no longer than 1 week.

——————— COOK'S HINT ———————

Don't despair! Should your mayonnaise curdle as a result of adding the oil too quickly too soon, here is a tip to rescue the mayonnaise. Put a fresh egg yolk into a clean basin, and very gradually whisk the curdled mixture into this. Then, continue as before.

AIOLI SAUCE

MAKES 300 ML (½ PINT)

1 quantity of Basic Mayonnaise
4 garlic cloves, crushed

salt and ground white pepper

Beat the crushed garlic into the mayonnaise. Season to taste. Cover and chill for at least 12 hours to allow the flavours to develop.

CURRIED MAYONNAISE

MAKES 300 ML (½ PINT)

1 quantity of Basic Mayonnaise
1 tablespoon medium hot curry powder
1 tablespoon mango chutney

1 teaspoon tomato purée
a dash of Tabasco sauce

Beat all the ingredients together thoroughly. Cover and chill for a couple of hours.

TARTARE SAUCE

MAKES 300 ML (½ PINT)

1 quantity of Basic Mayonnaise
2 tablespoons chopped capers
1 tablespoon chopped gherkins
1 spring onion, chopped finely

1 tablespoon chopped fresh parsley
1 tablespoon chopped fresh chives
1 hard-boiled egg, chopped coarsely
salt and ground white pepper

Fold all the ingredients together. Season to taste, cover and chill until required.

TOMATO MAYONNAISE

———————— MAKES 300 ML (½ PINT) ————————

½ quantity of Basic Mayonnaise
6 tablespoons whipping cream, lightly
whipped

3 tablespoons tomato purée
2 teaspoons Worcestershire sauce
salt and ground white pepper

Fold all the ingredients together. Season to taste, cover and chill until required.

THOUSAND ISLAND DIP

———————— MAKES APPROX 400 ML (14 FL OZ) ————————

1 quantity of Basic Mayonnaise
4 tablespoons tomato ketchup
4 tablespoons green olives, stoned and
chopped

2 tablespoons chopped fresh chives
1 tablespoon white wine vinegar
1 hard-boiled egg, chopped
salt and pepper

Mix all the ingredients together. Season to taste. Cover and chill.

GREEN GODDESS DRESSING

———————— MAKES APPROX 450 ML (¾ PINT) ————————

1 quantity of Basic Mayonnaise
6 tablespoons soured cream
4 canned anchovy fillets, drained and
chopped

1 tablespoon lemon juice
1 garlic clove, chopped finely
4 tablespoons chopped fresh parsley
salt and pepper

Place all the ingredients in a bowl and mix thoroughly. Season to taste.

CUCUMBER AND YOGURT DIP

———— MAKES 250 ML (8 FL OZ) ————

150 g (5 oz) natural yogurt
1 garlic clove, chopped finely
1 tablespoon white wine vinegar
½ cucumber, peeled, de-seeded and
chopped

2 tablespoons fresh chopped mint
salt and pepper
paprika for sprinkling

Place all the ingredients in a bowl and mix thoroughly. Season to taste. Cover and chill for at least 3 hours. Sprinkle some paprika over the surface before serving.

SOUR CREAM AND CHIVE DIP

———— MAKES 150 ML (¼ PINT) ————

150 ml (¼ pint) soured cream
4 tablespoons chopped fresh chives

salt and pepper

Mix all the ingredients together in a bowl. Season well. Cover and chill for 2 hours to allow the flavours to develop.

———— COOK'S HINT ————

To make your own soured cream, stir 2 teaspoons of lemon juice into 150 ml (¼ pint) double cream. Leave it, covered, to stand at room temperature for 15 minutes.

GARLIC DIP

———— MAKES 150 ML (¼ PINT) ————

1 medium-size onion, chopped finely
2 garlic cloves, crushed

150 ml (¼ pint) soured cream
salt and pepper

Mix all the ingredients together in a bowl. Season well. Cover and chill for 2 hours to allow the flavours to develop.
Pictured on page 82

AVOCADO DIP

—————— MAKES APPROX 250 ML (8 FL OZ) ——————

1 large ripe avocado, halved and stoned
1 tablespoon lemon juice
150 ml (¼ pint) soured cream
2 tablespoons mayonnaise

1 teaspoon Worcestershire sauce
1 teaspoon chopped fresh basil
salt and pepper

1 Spoon the avocado flesh into a bowl, scraping the inside of the shell thoroughly to include the darker green flesh.
2 Mash well (or purée in a food processor) together with the remaining ingredients. Check the seasoning. Cover and chill for 1 hour.

BLUE CHEESE DIP

—————— MAKES 150 ML (¼ PINT) ——————

6 tablespoons soured cream
75 g (3 oz) blue Stilton, or Danish
blue cheese, crumbled

1 tablespoon lemon juice
1 tablespoon chopped fresh chives
salt and pepper

Mix all the ingredients together in a bowl. Season to taste. Cover and chill for an hour to allow the flavours to develop.

—————— COOK'S HINT ——————

Rather than throwing out end pieces of blue cheese, pop them in the freezer and save them for crumbling into this dip.

PESTO SAUCE

—————————— *MAKES APPROX 150 ML (¼ PINT)* ——————————

25 g (1 oz) fresh basil leaves
4 garlic cloves
25 g (1 oz) pine kernels

50 g (2 oz) fresh parmesan cheese,
grated
125 ml (4 fl oz) olive oil
salt and pepper

1 In an electric blender or food processor, purée the basil, garlic, pine kernels and cheese together with 3 tablespoons of the olive oil.
2 Add the remaining oil, drop by drop, to form a smooth sauce. Season to taste with salt and pepper.

—————————— *COOK'S HINT* ——————————

This sauce will keep well for up to one week. Spoon into a clean jam jar then pour a very thin layer of olive oil on top to form a seal. Cover tightly and keep refrigerated. The sauce also freezes well.

MILD CURRY SAUCE

—————————— *MAKES 300 ML (½ PINT)* ——————————

1 medium-size onion, chopped finely
50 g (2 oz) butter
1 tablespoon mild curry powder
1 tablespoon plain flour
300 ml (½ pint) milk

2 tablespoons mango chutney
2 teaspoons desiccated coconut
(optional)
salt and pepper

1 In a saucepan, fry the onion in the butter until golden. Stir in the curry powder and cook for a minute. Blend in the flour and cook, stirring, for a further minute.
2 Gradually blend in the milk. Bring to the boil slowly and cook, stirring, until the sauce thickens.
3 Stir in the chutney and coconut (if using) and season with the salt and pepper. Serve warm.

QUICK HOLLANDAISE SAUCE

—————————— *MAKES 300 ML (½ PINT)* ——————————

Hollandaise sauce can be tricky and needs last-minute care and attention which can be a nightmare. Here's a quick method which will take just a few minutes to produce – and with no fear of curdling!

4 egg yolks
2 tablespoons water
2 tablespoons lemon juice

175 g (6 oz) butter, melted
a pinch of salt and white pepper

1 Put the egg yolks, water and lemon juice into a food processor or blender and turn on the motor.
2 While the machine is running, gradually pour in the melted warm butter, until the sauce becomes thick.
3 Season to taste and serve.

QUICK BÉARNAISE SAUCE

—————————— *MAKES APPROX 150 ML (¼ PINT)* ——————————

1 tablespoon chopped onion
2 tablespoons white wine or
tarragon vinegar
3 egg yolks
4 teaspoons lemon juice

150 g (5 oz) butter, melted
a pinch each of salt and ground black
pepper
1 tablespoon chopped tarragon or mint
(optional)

1 Put the onion and vinegar in a small saucepan and bring to the boil, reducing the vinegar by half. Strain the liquid and leave to cool.
2 Place the egg yolks and lemon juice in a food processor or blender and process until creamy. Add the strained vinegar, and, with the motor still running, gradually pour in the melted butter. The sauce will be thick and creamy.
3 Season to taste with the salt and pepper. Stir in the freshly chopped herbs, if using.

CUMBERLAND SAUCE

————— MAKES APPROX 200 ML (7 FL OZ) —————

6 tablespoons redcurrant jelly
3 tablespoons port
grated rind and juice of 1 orange

juice of 1 lemon
a pinch of dry mustard
a pinch of ground ginger

Heat all the ingredients together in a small saucepan, until the redcurrant jelly
has melted. Mix well, transfer to a serving bowl and leave to cool.
Pictured on page 82

SPICY TOMATO DIP

————— MAKES 200 ML (7 FL OZ) —————

3 tablespoons grated onion
3 tablespoons red wine vinegar
150 ml (¼ pint) tomato ketchup
1 teaspoon Worcestershire sauce

1 teaspoon caster sugar
½ teaspoon mild paprika
salt
1 tablespoon chopped fresh chives

1 Simmer the onion and vinegar together in a small pan for 3–4 minutes.
2 Remove from the heat and stir in the ketchup, Worcestershire sauce, caster
sugar and paprika. Season with a little salt.
3 Spoon into a serving bowl. Sprinkle on the chopped chives.

MINT RELISH

————— MAKES 125 ML (4 FL OZ) —————

4 tablespoons chopped fresh mint
2 tablespoons boiling water
1 teaspoon caster sugar
1 teaspoon mild paprika

6 tablespoons thick-set natural yogurt
1 spring onion, chopped finely
(optional)
salt

1 Place the mint in a bowl with the boiling water, sugar and half the paprika.
Mix well and leave to cool.
2 Whisk in the yogurt and chopped spring onion. Season to taste with salt.
3 Spoon into a small serving dish and sprinkle over the remaining paprika.

SWEET AND SOUR BARBECUE SAUCE

———————— *MAKES APPROX 600 ML (1 PINT)* ————————

2 tablespoons vegetable oil
1 medium-size onion, chopped finely
3 garlic cloves, chopped finely
1 kg (2 lb) tomatoes, peeled, de-seeded
and chopped
50 g (2 oz) soft brown sugar

4 tablespoons malt vinegar
2 tablespoons Worcestershire sauce
1 tablespoon tomato purée
1 tablespoon mild curry powder
salt and pepper

1 Heat the oil in a saucepan and fry the onion and garlic until softened.
2 Add the remaining ingredients, cover and simmer for 30 minutes, until thick. Check the seasoning.

———————— *COOK'S HINT* ————————

For a quick version, substitute 2 × 425 g (14 oz) cans of chopped tomatoes for the fresh tomatoes.

ORIENTAL SAUCE

———————— *MAKES 275 ML (9 FL OZ)* ————————

50 g (2 oz) soft brown sugar
4 tablespoons dark soy sauce
4 tablespoons dry sherry
4 tablespoons lemon juice

1 tablespoon apricot jam
2.5 cm (1-inch) piece of fresh ginger,
peeled and crushed
4 tablespoons vegetable oil

1 Place the sugar, soy sauce, sherry, lemon juice, jam and ginger in a small saucepan. Simmer for 5 minutes until the sugar and jam have dissolved.
2 Remove the ginger and discard. Whisk in the oil, until the sauce is smooth and glossy.
3 Cool slightly, before serving.

SWEET RED PEPPER SAUCE

MAKES APPROX 300 ML (½ PINT)

25 g (1 oz) butter
2 large sweet red peppers, de-seeded and chopped
1 shallot or ½ small onion, chopped finely

1 garlic clove, chopped finely
300 ml (½ pint) vegetable stock
a pinch of caster sugar
salt and pepper

1 Melt the butter in a small pan and add the red peppers, onion and garlic. Cover and cook for 5 minutes.
2 Pour on the stock and simmer, uncovered, for 10–15 minutes, until the red peppers are very tender.
3 Purée or sieve the sauce. Stir in the sugar and season to taste with salt and pepper. Serve warm.

RED PEPPER SAUCE WITH CHILLI

Make the sauce as above, and stir in 2 tablespoons of tomato ketchup, 2 teaspoons of red wine vinegar and 2 teaspoons of chilli sauce. Serve warm.
Pictured on page 71

COURT BOUILLON

MAKES 1.5 LITRES (2½ PINTS)

This flavoured stock can be used for fondues which require a good liquor for cooking the food in, and it can also go into soups and stews.

1.2 litres (2 pints) water
250 g (8 oz) carrots, chopped
1 large onion, sliced
1 celery stick, chopped

1 bouquet garni
8 black peppercorns, bruised lightly
1 bay leaf, broken
300 ml (½ pint) dry white wine

1 Put all the ingredients into a large saucepan and slowly bring to the boil.
2 Simmer for 1 hour, then strain and leave to cool.

ORANGE SAUCE

—————— MAKES APPROX 250 ML (8 FL OZ) ——————

Serve this orange sauce with the Orchard Fruits Fondue (page 97), and cinnamon cream – it can also be beaten into a pot of Greek yogurt to serve as an alternative but delicious dip.

2 large oranges
125 g (4 oz) fine-shred orange
marmalade
125 ml (4 fl oz) water

1 teaspoon icing sugar
1 teaspoon cornflour
15 g (½ oz) unsalted butter

1 Using a vegetable peeler, cut away the zest from one orange, taking care not to include the bitter white pith.
2 Cut the zest into very thin strips. Blanch in boiling water for 2 minutes, then drain and reserve.
3 Place the juice of 2 oranges, the marmalade and water in a small saucepan. Heat gently, stirring, until the marmalade has melted.
4 Press the sauce through a sieve and return to a clean pan. Stir in the icing sugar. Blend the cornflour with a little water to make a smooth paste and stir into the orange mixture.
5 Stir constantly over a moderate heat until the sauce is smooth and has thickened slightly. Remove from the heat, beat in the butter and stir in the reserved zest.
6 Serve warm or chilled.

FONDUE DIPPERS and DUNKERS

PARSLEY BISCUITS

MAKES APPROX. 38

Dried rosemary, marjoram or fennel seeds are good alternatives to the dried parsley in this recipe.

*150 g (5 oz) plain flour, plus extra
for rolling
125 g (4 oz) butter, diced
25 g (1 oz) lard, diced*

*1 teaspoon dried parsley
25 g (1 oz) onion, chopped finely
a little milk, to mix
salt*

1 Preheat the oven to Gas Mark 5/190°C/375°F. Lightly grease two large baking trays.
2 Sift the flour into a bowl. Add a pinch of salt. Rub the butter and the lard into the flour until the mixture resembles fine breadcrumbs. Stir in the parsley and chopped onion.
3 Add just enough milk to knead the mixture to a stiff dough. Turn onto a lightly floured surface and knead well.
4 Press the dough out to a thickness of 2 cm (¾ inch). Cut into small squares or triangles. Dust with a little extra flour.
5 Transfer the biscuits onto the baking trays and bake for 15–20 minutes until light golden.
6 Store in an airtight container for 2–4 days.

Pictured on page 89

GRUYÈRE MOONS

—————— MAKES APPROX. 30 ——————

This deliciously rich version of cheese straws comes from Switzerland.

175 g (6 oz) plain flour, plus extra for rolling
175 g (6 oz) unsalted butter, softened
175 g (6 oz) grated Gruyère cheese

1 egg, beaten, plus 1 yolk
a pinch of Cayenne pepper
salt

1 Preheat the oven to Gas Mark 4/180°C/350°C. Grease and flour two baking trays.
2 Mix together the flour and butter in a bowl, work in the cheese, the beaten egg and seasoning. Mix to a soft dough.
3 Cut the dough into two equal portions and chill one portion while rolling the other. Roll out the dough to 3 mm (⅛ inch) thick on a floured surface.
4 Cut into circles with a tumbler, then cut into each circle to make a crescent shape. Re-roll all the trimmings and re-cut until the dough is used up. Repeat with chilled portion.
5 Place on the baking trays. Beat the egg yolk and use to brush the tops. Bake for 8 minutes.

—————— COOKS HINT ——————

(You may like to freeze half the dough – seal in a polythene bag.)
Pictured on the front cover

SCHENKELI

—————— MAKES 20–25 ——————

These old-fashioned deep-fried Swiss pastries were traditionally served at carnival time, at local fairs or just on long winter evenings with friends. Delicious dipped into chocolate and fruit fondues, they are best eaten on the day they are made.

125 g (4 oz) white lard or shortening
150 g (5 oz) caster sugar
1 teaspoon of grated lemon peel
3 eggs, beaten

375 g (12 oz) plain flour, plus extra for rolling
¼ teaspoon baking powder
oil for frying

1 In a bowl, cream together the lard, sugar and lemon peel until light and fluffy. Gradually beat in the eggs.

2 Sift in the flour and baking powder and gradually fold in. Mix to a smooth dough.
3 Cut the dough into 20–25 small pieces, and press each piece out, on a floured surface, to form a 5–7-cm (2–3-inch) finger.
4 Score a line along the length of each finger with the tip of a pointed knife.
5 Heat enough oil for deep frying to 190°C/375°F. Deep fry the Schenkeli, a few at a time, until golden.
6 Drain on kitchen paper towels and leave to cool.

Pictured on page 118

PEANUT COOKIES

———————— *MAKES APPROX. 30* ————————

125 g (4 oz) caster sugar
75 g (3 oz) butter
2 tablespoons peanut butter
2 eggs, beaten

200 g (7 oz) self-raising flour
½ teaspoon ground allspice
125 g (4 oz) salted peanuts, chopped
finely

1 Preheat the oven to Gas Mark 5/190°C/375°F. Lightly grease two baking trays.
2 Cream together the sugar and butter until light and fluffy. Gradually work in the peanut butter and half the beaten egg.
3 Gradually add the flour and ground allspice and half the chopped peanuts. Stir well until blended.
4 Take small teaspoonfuls of the mixture and place well apart on a baking tray. Slightly flatten each cookie with a damp fork. Glaze the cookies by brushing with some of the remaining beaten egg. Sprinkle on the remaining nuts.
5 Bake for 20 minutes or until golden brown. Transfer to a wire rack to cool.

———————— *COOKS HINT* ————————

These cookies will store well in an airtight tin for two weeks.
Pictured on page 118

*Lemon Foam Fondue (page 103), with Schenkeli (page 116) and Peanut Cookies
(page 117)*

SAVOURY CHOUX PUFFS

MAKES APPROX. 100

These tiny puffs will store well in an airtight container for up to one week or, alternatively, keep them handy in the freezer. Reheat them in a moderate oven before serving, so that they will be crisp.

150 ml (¼ pint) water
50 g (2 oz) butter
75 g (3 oz) plain flour
a pinch of salt

2 eggs, beaten
25 g (1 oz) parmesan cheese, grated finely

1 Preheat the oven to Gas Mark 6/200°C/400°F. Slightly dampen two large baking trays.
2 Heat together the water and butter in a small saucepan. Remove from the heat and briskly beat in the flour and salt. Beat well until the mixture leaves the side of the pan and forms a ball of paste around the wooden spoon.
3 Add the eggs, a little at a time, beating thoroughly between each addition. The paste should now be glossy.
4 Stir in the cheese.
5 Spoon the mixture into a piping bag fitted with a 1 cm (½-inch) plain nozzle and pipe tiny mounds onto the baking trays, spacing them 2.5 cm (1 inch) apart.
6 Bake for 8–10 minutes until well risen and golden. Do not open the door during baking! Transfer to a wire rack to cool.

Pictured on page 35

SWEET CHOUX PUFFS

Follow the recipe and method as above, but replace the cheese with 1 teaspoon caster sugar. Lightly dust the cooked choux puffs with a little sifted icing sugar if serving immediately.

HERB CROUSTADES

Croustades are generally small bread or pastry cases, filled with a savoury cream or truffle filling. For fondues, small shells are ideal for dipping.

1 small brown or white french baguette,
sliced thinly
125 g (4 oz) butter, softened

2 tablespoons chopped fresh herbs
(parsley, chives, basil, dill)

1 Preheat the oven to Gas Mark 4/180°C/350°F.
2 Cream together the butter and herbs. Spread thinly on both sides of the bread slices.
3 Press the slices into small patty tins.
4 Bake in the oven for 15–20 minutes or until golden and crisp.
5 Leave to cool before transferring to an airtight container.

CURRIED BREAD CUBES

SERVES 6–8

Once made, these bread cubes will keep in an airtight container for up to one week. Wrap them in foil and warm through in a moderate oven before serving. They are delicious dipped into savoury cheese fondues.

1 small, unsliced, white loaf
75 g (3 oz) butter

2 tablespoons vegetable oil
1 tablespoon medium-hot curry powder

1 Remove the crusts from the loaf, cut the bread into 2-cm (¾-inch) slices, and then into 2-cm (¾-inch) cubes.
2 Heat the butter and oil together in a large frying pan. Stir in the curry powder.
3 Fry the bread cubes, stirring constantly, until golden brown and crisp. Drain on paper towels.

Pictured on page 35

COOKS HINT

To make Garlic Bread Cubes, follow the recipe and method above, but replace the curry powder with 4 crushed garlic cloves or 4 teaspoons of garlic granules.

Pictured on page 35

TOASTED CROÛTONS

For the calorie conscious, oven-baked croûtons make excellent dippers for a savoury fondue.
Preheat the oven to Gas Mark 4/180°C/350°F.
Remove the crusts from a small, unsliced white loaf and cut the bread into 2 cm (¾-inch) slices and then into 2 cm (¾-inch) cubes.
Place the cubes of bread onto a baking tray and heat in the oven for 10–15 minutes or until crisp and golden brown.
To add a hint of garlic, rub the bread slices with a cut garlic clove, before cutting into cubes.
Toasted croûtons will keep well for two weeks in an airtight container.

IRISH SODA BREAD

———————— MAKES 1 LARGE LOAF ————————

Irish soda bread does not use yeast, but relies on the reaction between the bicarbonate of soda and buttermilk to raise the dough. If you do not have buttermilk, use ordinary milk 'soured' with 2 tablespoons of lemon juice. It is best eaten on the day it is made.
The scored cross on the dough helps with the rising, although the Irish may tell you it is to let the fairies out!

500 g (1 lb) plain flour, plus extra for rolling
1 level teaspoon sugar
1 level teaspoon salt

1 level teaspoon bicarbonate of soda
scant 450 ml (¾ pint) buttermilk
oil for greasing

1 Preheat the oven to Gas Mark 7/220°C/425°F. Lightly oil a large baking sheet.
2 Sift the dry ingredients into a bowl and make a well in the centre.
3 Pour most of the milk in and quickly work in the flour to form a soft, not too wet, sticky dough. Add a little more milk if necessary.
4 On a well-floured surface, shape the dough into a round loaf about 4 cm (1½ inches) deep. Score a deep cross into the loaf.
5 Bake for 35–40 minutes or until cooked. Tap the bottom of the bread; if it sounds hollow, the loaf is cooked.

MACAROONS

These delicious biscuits will store well in an airtight container for two weeks, or alternatively freeze well. Variations are also given for coconut macaroons and Petits Fours.

200 g (7 oz) ground almonds
150 g (5 oz) caster sugar
2 egg whites
½ teaspoon vanilla essence

20 whole blanched almonds
TO GLAZE:
1 tablespoon icing sugar
2 tablespoons milk

1 Lightly grease and line 2 large baking trays with silicone paper. Preheat the oven to Gas Mark 4/180°C/350°F.
2 Mix together the ground almonds and sugar.
3 In a large bowl, beat the egg whites until frothy and light. Stir in the almond mixture and vanilla essence.
4 Spoon the mixture into a large piping bag with a large plain tube. Pipe 5 cm (2-inch) rounds onto the baking sheets. Top each macaroon with a whole almond.
5 Bake for 15–20 minutes until just golden brown.
6 Heat together the icing sugar and milk in a small saucepan and brush this glaze over the hot macaroons.
7 Carefully transfer the macaroons to a wire rack to cool.

Pictured on page 63

——————— COOKS HINT ———————

To make Coconut Macaroons: substitute 75 g (3 oz) desiccated coconut for the ground almonds and decorate each macaroon with a piece of glacé cherry, instead of an almond.
Pictured on page 43
To make Petits Fours: follow the method for macaroons, but pipe 2.5 cm (1-inch) rosettes, S-shapes and hearts onto the silicone paper. Bake for 10–12 minutes. Makes 50.

Pictured on page 63

ESKIMO BANANAS

——— SERVES 6 ———

These banana 'lollies' are great fun for children to dip into a dessert fondue. Do remember to remove them from the freezer half an hour before serving.

6 small firm bananas
2 tablespoons lemon juice
125 g (4 oz) white chocolate, melted

coloured hundreds and thousands
6 cocktail or lollipop sticks

1 Line a baking tray with greaseproof or silicone paper.
2 Peel and cut each banana in half. Toss in the lemon juice and pat dry on a piece of kitchen paper towel.
3 Insert a cocktail or lollipop stick into the cut end of each banana half.
4 Dip the bananas in the melted chocolate, to coat the top half of each.
5 Sprinkle hundreds and thousands over the chocolate. Carefully lay each banana lolly on the baking tray.
6 Freeze for 1 hour, to set. Half an hour before serving, transfer the eskimo bananas to the refrigerator.

AMERICAN AND AUSTRALIAN CONVERSION CHART

	BRITISH	AMERICAN	AUSTRALIAN
Teaspoons and tablespoons	1 teaspoon (5 ml)	1 teaspoon (5 ml)	1 teaspoon (5 ml)
	*1 tablespoon	1 rounded tablespoon	1 scant tablespoon
	2 tablespoons	2 tablespoons	1½ tablespoons
	3 tablespoons	3 tablespoons	2½ tablespoons
	4 tablespoons	4 tablespoons	3½ tablespoons
	5 tablespoons	5 tablespoons	4½ tablespoons
†*Cup measures –* *liquid*	4 tablespoons	¼ cup	¼ cup
	125 ml (4 fl oz)	½ cup	½ cup
	250 ml (8 fl oz)	1 cup	1 cup
	450 ml (¾ pint)	2 cups	2 cups
	600 ml (1 pint)	2½ cups	2½ cups
Cup measures – *solid*	250 g (8 oz) butter	1 cup	1 cup
	250 g (8 oz) grated cheese	2 cups	2 cups
	2 medium onions, chopped	1 cup	1 cup
	125 g (4 oz) sliced mushrooms	½ cup	½ cup
	250 g (8 oz) flour	2 cups	2 cups
	50 g (2 oz) breadcrumbs	½ cup	½ cup

British standard tablespoon=15 ml; American standard tablespoon=14.2 ml; Australian standard tablespoon=20 ml.
†*American measuring cup=250 ml (8 fl oz); Australian measuring cup=250 ml (8 fl oz).*
(Note: British pint=20 fl oz; American pint=16 fl oz; Australian pint=20 fl oz)

LE CREUSET FONDUE RANGE

Free Helpline: If you have any questions about Le Creuset (before or after you buy) call Le Creuset free – we will be delighted to help. Dial 0800 37–37–92 (Monday to Friday 10 a.m.–4 p.m.), UK only.

10 year guarantee: All Le Creuset products are guaranteed for ten years against failures caused by faulty materials or workmanship. This guarantee does not affect your statutory rights and is valid for ten years.

6001 Dual-Function Fondue Set
Enamelled cast iron pot
6 forks
Le Creuset Firestar burner

1¼ pint maximum oil level

6071 Dual-Function Fondue Set
Enamelled cast iron stand,
pot and fork holding cover
6 forks
Le Creuset Firestar burner

1¼ pint maximum oil level

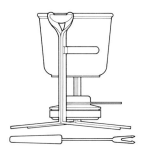

6081 Oval Dual-Function Fondue Set
Enamelled cast iron pot
Black cast iron stand
6 forks
Le Creuset Firestar burner

1¼ pint maximum oil level

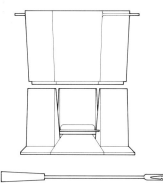

3621 Hexagonal Dual-Function Fondue Set
Enamelled cast iron pot
Black cast iron stand
6 forks
Le Creuset Firestar burner

1¼ pint maximum oil level

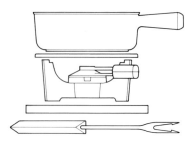

6034 Dual-Function Fondue Set
Black cast iron stand
Enamelled cast iron pot with
phenolic insulated handles
Fork holding cover
6 forks
Le Creuset Firestar burner

1 ¼ pint maximum oil level

3610 Cheese Fondue Set
Enamelled cast iron pot with side
handle
Black cast iron stand with cork mat
6 forks
Alcohol burner

3 ½ pint maximum melted cheese
level

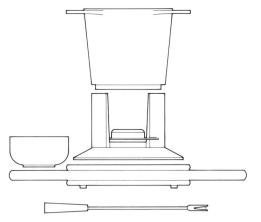

6800 Chocolate Fondue Set
Enamelled cast iron pot
Black cast iron stand with wooden
tray
4 forks
Candle heater

½ pint maximum melted chocolate
level

Le Creuset wooden Fondue
Turntable with 6 earthenware
crudité/dips dishes

6570 Pack of 6 Fondue forks

6590 Pack of 3 Le Creuset Firestar
Plus refills

6610 Firestar burner including one
tin of Le Creuset Firestar paste

6580 Alcohol Burner

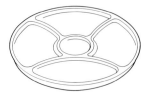

9112 White earthenware sectioned
Fondue plate

INDEX